CREATING YOUR BEST YOU

LOSE THE OVERWHELM—

USE THIS STEP-BY-STEP PROCESS TO GAIN CLARITY AND LIVE YOUR HAPPIEST LIFE

JOS GIEZEMAN

Creating Your Best You: Lose the Overwhelm – Use this Step-by-Step Process to Gain Clarity and Live Your Happiest Life
By Jos Giezeman

Published by Jos Giezeman

Cover and Interior Design by Victoria Wolf, wolfdesignandmarketing.com
Photography by Photography G, Inc., photographyg.com
Editing by Patrice Rhoades-Baum of Sojourn Enterprises, www.PatriceRB.com
Publishing support by Aaron Schafer at Self-PublishingSchool.com.

ISBN: 978-1-7378933-1-8

Publisher's Cataloging-in-Publication data

Names: Giezeman, Jos, author.
Title: Creating your best you : lose the overwhelm - use this step-by-step process to gain clarity and live your happiest life / by Jos Giezeman.
Description: Denver, CO: Jos Giezeman, 2021.
Identifiers: LCCN: 2021922510 | ISBN: 978-1-7378933-2-5 (hardcover) | 978-1-7378933-1-8 (paperback) | 978-1-7378933-0-1 (ebook)
Subjects: LCSH Self-actualization (Psychology). | Happiness. | Conduct of life. | Time management. | Habit. | Performance. | Self-help. | BISAC SELF-HELP / Personal Growth / Happiness | SELF-HELP / Time Management. | BUSINESS & ECONOMICS / Time Management.
Classification: LCC BF637.T5 .G54 2021 | DDC 646.7--dc23

Library of Congress Control Number: 2021922510

To order the book or learn more about the author, visit www.CreatingYBY.com

To Kathy —
my soulmate, best friend, and translator
together with whom one-plus-one magically equals three

CONTENTS

3: CONNECTING YOUR PRESENT & FUTURE

PROLOGUE

Feeling overwhelmed? Here's why you want to read this book ...

THIS BOOK OFFERS YOU THE OPPORTUNITY to take command of your life. Up to now, you may have been living your life from day to day and getting by — instinctively hoping you will end up someplace decent. I believe you have a better option.

In essence, this book helps you by focusing your energy on the one resource you have that is not renewable: *your time*. It is my intent that you understand the value and the step-by-step process of Creating Your Best You after only thirty *hours* or so — rather than the thirty *years* it took me. This book will show you a simple and systematic way to organize common sense into your common practice. Over time, this will produce impressive results in those areas of life that most matter to you.

My inspiration for developing this process came from realizing that if my life is more important to me than my company, then why am I so much clearer on what I need to do with my company than with myself? For our business, together with the whole leadership team, we had created a clear game plan. Everyone knew who, what, when, how, and why we did our work. With the increased clarity, our company took off and quickly grew, exceeding our wildest expectations. Yet I was much less clear about my own game plan. Could I apply what I had learned for my business to my personal life? Could I clarify my who, what, when, how, and why to create the best, most fulfilled version of myself?

The process described in this book helped me to create balance and achieve success in *both* my personal and professional life. Today, I live my life with a sense of purpose. Once I create my Weekly Plan, I experience a deep sense of peace of mind and can be more fully present in the moment, knowing that all the important parts of my life will get my focused attention during this week. Even when I take "me" time I can do so without feeling guilty.

The key to this process is making small but steady improvements every week in the areas that are most important to me. When I look back, I feel a sense of amazement and awe at how these small steps over the years created mega leaps forward. Naturally, life would sometimes throw me off course, but the routine of following my life masterplan would help me to get back on track quickly and achieve what I had chosen as my most important priorities.

When friends, or even acquaintances, hear about my success and satisfaction with both my family and business and see the clarity I have in my life, they almost always ask for more details. They sense I am clear on what I want and why that is important to me. When I act accordingly, when I "walk the talk," it shows integrity and generates trust more easily. Frequently, I am asked to provide personal coaching on the underlying process that helped to create these results.

Over the years I slowly learned how little control I actually have. In the end, the only piece of my life I can control is *me*. I realized that whatever changes I wanted to make in my life and my environment, I needed to start with *me* and work from the inside out. Since what I can control is so little, I learned to maximize this power by becoming crystal clear about my life's priorities and to design and execute my game plan to achieve these priorities. I need that kind of clarity to make the right choices at critical junctures in my personal and professional life.

I began to step through a process to clarify my life's purpose, develop my life masterplan, create the best person I could be, and live my happiest life. This process resulted in greater simplicity and transparency for myself, which helped me to make great choices. Along the way, I developed an easy, day-by-day method to connect my current activities to my future goals. And each week, I narrowed the gap between where I was and where I wanted to be. Over time, I began to feel the steady progress of living my life more intentionally!

I have always been inspired by the "inside out" wisdom of the inscription on the tomb of an English bishop who lived in the eleventh century:

> *"When I was young and free and my imagination had no limits, I dreamed of changing the world. As I grew older and wiser, I discovered the world would not change. So, I shortened my sights somewhat and decided to change only my country, but it too seemed immovable. As I grew into my twilight years, in one desperate attempt, I settled for changing only my family, those closest to me, but alas, they too would have none of it. And now*

I realize as I lie on my deathbed, if I had only changed myself first, then by example I might have changed my family. From their inspiration and encouragement, I would have been able to better my country, and who knows, I might have even changed the world."

Over the years, I've honed this process, which I now call Creating Your Best You. As I share this process with you, I will illustrate each step with personal examples including some successes and some of the many mistakes I have made. My journey begins with my moment of truth.

CHAPTER 1

MY MOMENT OF TRUTH

I LAY IN BED, motionless in my darkened bedroom, wearing a mask to keep out every bit of light. Everything in the room was still, and I was so focused and afraid that I could even smell the damp air permeating from the crawl space below our cheap rental house. The sound of the traffic in front of our house on Ella Street became magnified as the high school across the street was about to ring its last bell for the day. The slightest noise, light, or movement was excruciatingly painful.

Earlier that afternoon at the hospital emergency room in our small rural town, Doctor Dan, my family doctor, had ordered an emergency CT scan of my brain. The nurse injected me with radiological contrast material that would allow the physician to determine the presence of an aneurysm or brain tumor. She patiently tightened all the screws on the band around my head to prevent any movement while I was inside the narrow opening of the CT scanner. I closed my eyes in a futile attempt to hide from the pain in my head as the flashing red lights at the opening of the scanner were still clearly visible on my optic nerves.

The rolling bed tray I was lying on slid slowly into the claustrophobic, circular space. I tried to focus on steadying my breathing as the rhythmic, metallic clacks of the camera took sliced pictures of my brain, aggravating the headache further. Having never experienced anything remotely like this headache, I now really started to worry. What was wrong with my brain? A tumor? Some sort of cancer? An aneurysm? How would my wife Kathy raise our two-year-old son Adam by herself and run the company too? How would this all play out?

As I stared at the round, white ceiling inside the CT scanner I knew I had to make some big changes in my life. Working well over 100 hours a week, giving everything I had to our company while frequently eating pizza dinners or other quick meals, then washing it all down with a few cold beers was clearly not the way to live. *I guess I am not invincible after all* I thought to myself. Right then and there, I made the solemn promise that if I somehow survived this crisis, I would figure out a way to live my life much healthier and more balanced. But how long would I have to wait before Doctor Dan could give me the test results — and what would the test find?

CHAPTER 2

LEADING UP TO MY CRASH

THAT HEALTH SCARE WAS IN EARLY 1986, and I was twenty-eight years old. Kathy and I had just started our company six months earlier, having purchased Searcy Laundry, a sixty-year-old uniform, linen, and family laundry business in Searcy, Arkansas. The former owners had reached retirement age and were ready to sell.

We'd bought the company with our life savings of $15,000 and a creative combination of different types of loans totaling $1,000,000. Prime loan rates were twelve percent, and with our huge debt, our interest rates were well above those prime rate levels. After our first week's payroll, we had less than five dollars left in our company's checking account.

Since that first week, making our interest and principal payments had been a monthly adventure. The company we bought was tired and worn out. All the delivery trucks were older than ten years, the laundry equipment was older than fifteen years, and a much-needed office computer system was never installed. The original building from the 1920s was still standing, but a dozen lean-to additions had been added as more space was needed.

Scary as all that was for us, by far the most nerve-wracking situation was the fact that the antiquated laundry equipment had been changed-up over the years. We had no idea how to keep this old equipment going. I knew management, not machines. The only expert was the company's lone maintenance man, Jim, who had just turned in his resignation notice a few days before the severe pain in my head had started!

Back at the hospital, the staff expedited the processing of the CT scanner test results and, after a few hours, Doctor Dan returned with the results: there was no tumor, cancer, or any sign of an aneurysm! Just a serious migraine caused by work stress and unhealthy living. He told me to go home, rest, and cut out all processed foods, salt, spices, caffeine, and alcohol. I did not care what I had to do; I was elated and grateful for having received this second chance.

After resting at home in bed for the remainder of the week and following a strict diet, the migraine slowly subsided. On Monday, when I returned to work, I tackled the most critical issue first. After my long plea and a big pay increase, our lone maintenance guy decided to stay on for a while longer.

When my parents, who still lived in the Netherlands like the rest of my family, heard the news of my migraine, they decided it was time to step up. They quickly flew over to babysit Adam, cook meals, and do whatever else they could to help our household. Eventually, with lots of help and some good luck, the migraines stayed away, the laundry equipment kept running, and my life returned slowly to some level of normality.

Now that my most urgent problems were back under control, I knew I needed to take a hard look at my life, zoom out with a helicopter view, and reinvent a game plan for my company, my family, and especially myself. Deep down inside, I felt confident that I would come up with a game plan to make these massive changes in my life, because I'd done it before.

CHAPTER 3

MY CHILDHOOD TRANSITION

I WAS BORN AND RAISED in the Netherlands, and for as long as I can remember, I stuttered — a lot. When I started in the all-boys elementary school at the Catholic Saint Bavo School, I became more and more sensitive about my stuttering. Afraid of how I sounded, I tried hard to stay away from situations in which I would stutter. I tried to avoid saying anything at all, and when I did speak, I attempted to replace words that gave me trouble with easier words. For instance, one kilogram with the difficult K sound became two pounds. It mostly led to more confusing sentences and more insecurity.

During my early school years, my dad told me that sooner or later I would just grow out of this stuttering. I could not wait for that to happen! All through elementary and especially later in high school, I wished I could speak like everyone else. What the heck was taking so long?

I continued to try and find ways to compensate for my disability. I remember figuring out each teacher's method for asking students to read a section of text out loud. As I calculated my future reading assignment, I started to see all the difficult words I would have to pronounce. Of course, by the time it was finally my turn, so much tension had built up that I could not even read three words in two minutes. I felt embarrassed and frustrated in front of my teacher and all my classmates. There were times when teachers asked a question of the whole class and no one knew the answer except me. However, there was no way I would raise my hand and volunteer for yet another stuttering experience. Of course, afterward I felt even angrier at myself for not trying. I felt boxed in on all sides.

When it was especially important for me to speak well, like when I needed to talk to an authority figure or a pretty girl, the stuttering always got even worse than normal. I was angry and upset at myself and the world at large. At night I prayed to God to make a trade: He could take my arms or my legs, if He just let me speak like the other kids.

Then the unthinkable happened. I was fifteen years old in the tenth grade, helping after hours in the school library with a few friends. My Dutch language teacher, Mr. Van Der Pol, was there as the librarian in charge. On this particular day, Mr. Van Der Pol told me casually, as if it were a matter of fact, that since I was still stuttering at this age, I would most likely stutter for the rest of my life. I was devastated. What happened to being patient and waiting to grow out of this misery? It felt like my future life dreams were evaporating in front of me as I pictured myself stuttering for the rest of my life. I cried as I slowly pedaled my bicycle home from school.

After I explained to my parents what had happened that day, we all agreed the "growing out of it" time was now officially over. It was time to get help. Initially, I worked with two well-meaning family friends who had also stuttered earlier in their lives but, ultimately, I ended up with a professional teacher and former singer, Mrs. Serlee. She lived in The Hague, an hour train ride away. Early every Saturday morning for the next handful of years, we worked on breathing and throat exercises, but mostly we just talked. When I was comfortable and did not think about stuttering or when I attempted to sing, I found that I did not stutter. Amazing! We talked about breathing and being positive, and we worked on my confidence.

A few months later, I told her that later in the year the family would celebrate my grandparents' forty-fifth wedding anniversary. My Opa and Oma (Dutch for grandfather and grandmother) had twelve children, and a huge party was planned with over a hundred family members in attendance. There would be a five-course, sit-down dinner with dancing afterward and, of course, lots of speeches during dinner.

My Uncle Henk was the party's lead organizer, and he challenged me that as the oldest grandchild and *stamhouder* (literally "he who holds the family tree trunk"), I should give a speech representing all the grandchildren. He then said it was up to me. If I did not want to give the speech, he told me he would just ask the next oldest, Marjolein. I could not let that happen! I was the oldest grandchild, and I loved my Opa and Oma. No, I just had to do this speech.

Saying yes to giving the grandchildren's speech felt good at that moment, but I quickly became scared to death. Why in the world had I agreed to give that speech? I would be the first speaker while the waiters served the soup course. All I could picture was everyone politely waiting and then having to eat cold soup by the time I was finally done stuttering through my speech.

We had almost six months to prepare, and with input from Mrs. Serlee, I wrote and rewrote the speech. After several weeks, I ended up with a short, heartfelt, and funny presentation. I felt great about the content of the speech, and now all that was left was presenting it. Over the next months, I spent hundreds of hours practicing my speech. Every word, every intonation, every pause, every facial expression was rehearsed until I absolutely knew it by heart. Most important, I felt my confidence growing. Maybe I could pull off this speech after all.

On the big day I was extremely nervous. I had hardly eaten all day. The room felt immense, and my table was all the way in the back. Everyone was asked to sit down since dinner was about to start. As the waiters began to serve the warm soup, Uncle Henk announced that I wanted to speak on behalf of the grandchildren. I remember slowly rising from my chair, standing up straight at my table and taking deep breaths as my heart pounded furiously. There I stood, in front of more than a hundred family members who all seemed as anxious as I was. However, I was so focused on the presentation — with all the expressions, pauses, and intonations — and I knew the words so well, that the speaking itself went perfectly. No stuttering at all and the soup was still warm when everyone went back to eating! I felt such a relief and found myself shaking.

The main thing I clearly remember was Oma immediately standing up in her long white gown and walking in between all the dinner tables. She had tears rolling down her cheeks as she made her way to the back of the room to give me a big hug.

Now I knew I could do anything if I just prepared and practiced. This speech was the first of many more speeches to come at family events and at Nyenrode Business University as the chairman of the rugby club. With each successful speech, I grew more confident and gained the strength to hold that fearful beast of stuttering at bay.

After graduating from college in the Netherlands, I was invited to participate in a one-year exchange student MBA program at the

University of Georgia. On my twenty-first birthday, I left my home country, family, and friends, and flew to the U.S. Of course, I was nervous about all the unknowns in this new country, but I was also delighted and full of energy. Coming to the U.S. was like being given a clean slate, as if my past was washed away. No one knew about this "angry at the world" stuttering boy. Everyone in the U.S. knew me for what they saw right then and there: the new and improved me. Even speaking a new language without that difficult Dutch word history was a gift. I loved being in this country for all the opportunities I could envision here and this chance to reinvent myself.

After having successfully fought my way through my stuttering challenges, I felt that if I just prepared, practiced, and worked hard enough, I could overcome any challenge I would encounter in the future. I realized I am not confined to a predestined path for my life. If I did not like where my life was headed, the key to transitioning to a better future was there all along: it was within me.

CHAPTER 4

MY BUSINESS TRANSITION

DURING THAT MOMENT OF TRUTH medical wake-up call, I realized it was quite amazing how my body told me so clearly that I was screwing up. It let me know that I had to change big and change quickly. While I started to live a more balanced life by eating better, drinking less, and exercising in early morning workouts, I actually was doing just enough to avoid my next health crisis. In effect, I was putting a Band-Aid on each health issue rather than creating an overall plan. My real passion at the time was to develop a comprehensive game plan to lead our company through this crucial stage with us as new owners and its first real leadership team. Looking back, I can now see how going through my childhood and business transitions helped me to create my life transition and life masterplan.

The preparation, practice, and work to build our company game plan came in many different pieces. Devouring business books helped me learn the importance of narrowing our company's focus and providing just one world-class service rather than half a dozen average services. Within the first quarter of owning our business, we sold off most of our product lines — linen supply, dry cleaning, and family laundry — and focused solely on uniform rentals. Our revenue took a significant hit, but now our focus was clear. With much better systems and a simpler organization, we returned to the same sales volume by the end of the following year. The rapid growth in our uniform rental business created another learning opportunity, clearly demonstrating the need for a masterplan for our plant layout. By having a long-range plan, we would avoid mistakes such as moving a machine to a "perfect place," only to wish a few months later that we had placed it ten feet in another direction to allow for even more machines. We hired a leadership team, and we all took several management classes at the local Harding University. Together we worked to implement our new learning in our company.

Perhaps the biggest step in developing our company game plan was when we hired an industry consultant from San Francisco to help us create our first strategic business plan. After the first planning meeting at our location, the consultant informed me that it took him so long to travel to our plant in rural Arkansas that he refused to go there again. He decided instead to teach me the strategic planning process over the phone, so I could then teach the rest of our leadership team.

As it turned out, the consultant did me a huge favor as I discovered how much deeper I ended up learning the material as a teacher. Formulating our business strategic plan with well-defined values, mission, and vision showed me the power of creating a clear picture and direction for the whole team.

This led to the creation of our weekly management report, which measured all key result areas. Each Monday we produced a detailed report based on last week's activities and results. All key areas of the company were compared to their goals and discussed in our weekly Tuesday morning leadership meetings. This weekly follow-up system provided accountability and kept our strategic plan alive by connecting our values, mission, vision, and annual goals to our weekly results and day-to-day lives.

The final piece of the company game plan was developing a clear culture. I believe creating the right culture is perhaps the most important job of the top leadership in a company. Our leadership team spent time seeking answers to these types of questions:

- What are our values, principles, and beliefs for how we act in our company?
- How do people act when there are no clear instructions?
- What do they do when I am not around?

Returning from a quarterly business meeting with industry peers and stranded in the Nashville airport late one night, I discovered Stephen Covey's book, *The 7 Habits of Highly Effective People.* As I read his book, I had to put it down every few pages to take a breather, as the timing was so perfect for the information it offered. His book showed me a systematic way to create high-trust relationships and the importance of character, competence, and integrity. Covey's book was the key to clarifying our company culture and leadership language.

We could not afford to send all our teammates to Covey's three-day seminar, so I became a licensed trainer for Covey's leadership courses and trained our teammates on site. Of course, this also meant I needed to model the behavior I was looking for in our teammates. One example of how our culture began to evolve was that working on the weekends became a sign of failure. As a leader you could work on Friday nights until midnight, if necessary, but you could not show up for work on Saturdays or Sundays. We all needed to be away from work on the weekends in order to keep our lives in balance and to recharge our batteries, so we could be fresh and ready to go on Monday mornings.

As a result of all I had come to know as it related to our business, I began to ask myself some deeper questions. Why was creating a clear business game plan so normal, yet so few of us create a clear game plan for our personal lives? If our lives and our families are as important as our businesses, why wouldn't we apply the same dedication and principles to create a life masterplan?

Ultimately, my simple revelation was that it made just as much sense to create a masterplan for my life as it did for my business. I realized too, that I needed to do this before the next crisis happened. With a clear plan, I would lose the overwhelm and gain clarity. I would know which direction to take when that next unexpected fork in the road appeared.

CHAPTER 5

MY LIFE TRANSITION

OVER TIME, my life masterplan evolved into the tools and practices I still use today. Even in retirement, the process I established and refined over many years still works for me in my day-to-day living — and my ability to work toward and achieve a wide variety of life goals such as writing this book.

Creating my life masterplan and executing on this plan each week for the last thirty years has made a magnificent impact on both my professional and personal life. As a result, I feel extremely grateful, thrilled, and energized by my life. I'm forty years into a terrific marriage, I'm close to our three adult children who are making their own mark on the world, and I have wonderful relationships with extended family and friends. Exercise has become an almost daily habit, and I keep learning and studying by reading a different book every week or two. I eat and drink much more mindfully, and there are no more migraines!

Our business became enormously successful. Kathy and I sold it after seventeen years and retired in our mid-forties — almost twenty years ago. Sure, there was a ton of good luck involved. But we also implemented a systematic process that we continued to optimize, leading to great outcomes personally and professionally, again and again.

Up to now, you may have been living your life from month to month or even day to day, perhaps making a left turn here, followed by a right one there, and then a left turn again. You may feel as though you are barely keeping your head above water and sometimes feel like just throwing your hands up in despair. Most likely, you are regularly faced with urgent decisions and are making the best choices you can in the moment. But do you have a sneaking suspicion you have not thought everything through? Are you just trying to find a way to get by, blindly hoping it leads somewhere good? I am here to tell you this: You don't have to continue to be dragged along by life in this way.

This book offers you the opportunity to take control of your life. It will show you a new way to organize commonsense pieces into a coherent, practical, step-by-step process. One step at a time, you'll discover how to produce dramatic, consistent results week after week in all the areas of your life that matter most to you. You can apply company success components such as values, follow-up actions, and a clear picture of the desired future to your personal life. I believe the value of what is presented here lies in its simplicity — it is how to make common sense your common practice.

I am excited to share these insights in order to genuinely help you along the path of your life. It is my intention that by the end of this book you too can use this step-by-step process to identify and improve all the important parts of your life — and find your life in balance with peace of mind. Especially when measured over the years, the consistency of the direction and the regular improvements in areas that matter most to you make this process so powerful. Let's get started by taking the first step toward creating your life masterplan. In the following chapters, we'll step through a simple process for Creating Your Best You, so you can live your life to the fullest and happiest.

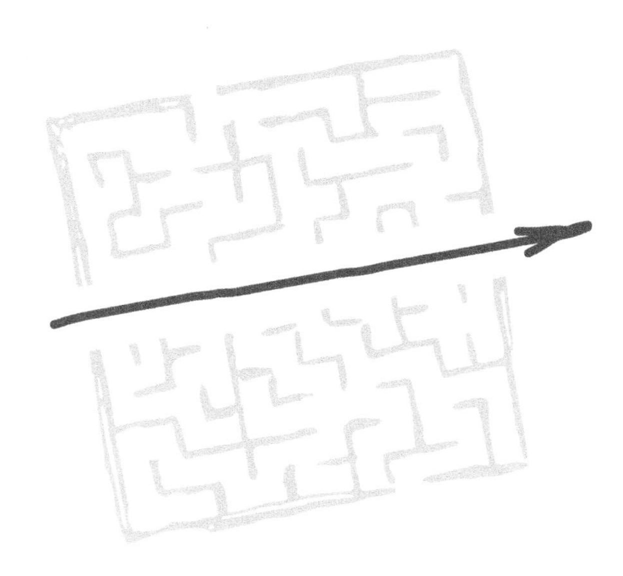

1: YOUR PRESENT

CHAPTER 6

INTRODUCTION

START BY CLARIFYING YOUR PRESENT SITUATION

WHEN I THINK BACK about the time before I used my life masterplan and had not truly clarified what was important to me, I instantly recall a feeling of being overwhelmed. I remember always being so busy and feeling swamped with the demands of getting our small company off the ground, spending time with our growing family (now with three kids), taking on leadership roles at church and in the community, coaching and attending soccer games and practices, and taking time for extended family visits. *Phew!* I get tired just remembering those days!

Creating your life masterplan consists of three major sections:

1. Improving your *present* situation.
2. Picturing clearly your desired *future* situation.
3. Steadily working to connect both positions over time through a systematic *weekly* process using your customized Weekly Planner.

In this first section covering Chapters 6 through 14, I will describe what worked for me to make small, consistent improvements once I had clearly decided what was most important to me. I will share my experiences and examples of how I could immediately improve my present situation once I had more clarity on what I really wanted.

I was very busy doing pretty *good* work. In order to make room in my life for *great* work, I needed greater clarity on exactly what was important to me. That way I could more easily and accurately assign a high or low importance value to each of my activities. So, what was deeply important to me? What was so dear to me I would risk my life to protect it? What did I value most in my life?

Throughout this section, I will share my favorite exercises and personal examples to help you create this clarity for yourself. Using these tools, you can immediately put your new insights to work in your everyday life. Together, let's take these first steps toward helping you gain clarity and live your happiest life.

CHAPTER 7

"HELP ME FREE UP SOME TIME FIRST, BEFORE I CAN EVEN THINK ABOUT CREATING A PLAN!"

TIME IS EVERYTHING. *Every … Single… Thing. Time is the only thing in the universe that is not renewable. Either you use it wisely or you do not.*

Even after the warning signs, the emergency room visit, and my good intentions, my lifestyle changes were certainly not an overnight success. Looking back, I can now see that I started by making just enough changes to stay out of health and family troubles, so I could continue to focus on my company.

As the owner of a small, fast-growing business, I still ended up with too many weeks of working excessive hours. As the company continued to grow and we hired our leadership team and outside salesforce,

I was the type of owner who put himself smack in the middle of most questions, problems, and changes. I tried to handle whatever issue someone brought to me as quickly as possible. If I could not do it now, I would write it down on my yellow pad — adding and crossing off items all day long. If you wanted to talk to me, you needed to wait in line outside my office or walk with me through the backdoor of the plant to Main Street Café for a quick working lunch.

Even though I was jumping from one crisis to the next, I felt important, as if I were making a difference — and sometimes even felt quite productive. But I also had this nagging feeling something was not quite right and wondered how sustainable my methods were as we continued to grow our business.

Then there was all this other life stuff besides work: family, friends, exercising, church, and so on. By this time, we had three children and Kathy rightly insisted that no matter how busy we were at the company, we would have a family dinner around 6:00 every evening. If I still had important work left to do by the end of the day, I would finish it by going to work early the next morning. That meant skipping my morning exercise routine of "NordicTrack skiing while reading a business book."

Throughout this time, we were also coaching all three of our kids' soccer teams. Since I spoke with a Dutch accent in rural Arkansas, I had instant credibility as a soccer coach! I did the coaching part and Kathy handled all other team details. Despite all my efforts, I almost always felt guilty about how I was spending my time and worried there were parts of my life that did not get enough attention. I was doing as much as I could while continually rearranging the priorities on my daily to-do lists based on the immediate crisis. Not only was I always short on time, but how could I know I was choosing the right activities for the time I did have?

Stephen Covey's *The 7 Habits of Highly Effective People* helped by introducing me to a new tool to look at all my activities, which he calls the Time Management Matrix. Interestingly, President Dwight D. Eisenhower initially created this time management tool many decades ago. Now known as the Eisenhower Matrix, this tool helped him to focus on the most important tasks of the day. This tool presents a simple diagram to help you evaluate each activity based on only two components: the task's importance and the task's urgency, with each rated high or low. This generates four different quadrants.

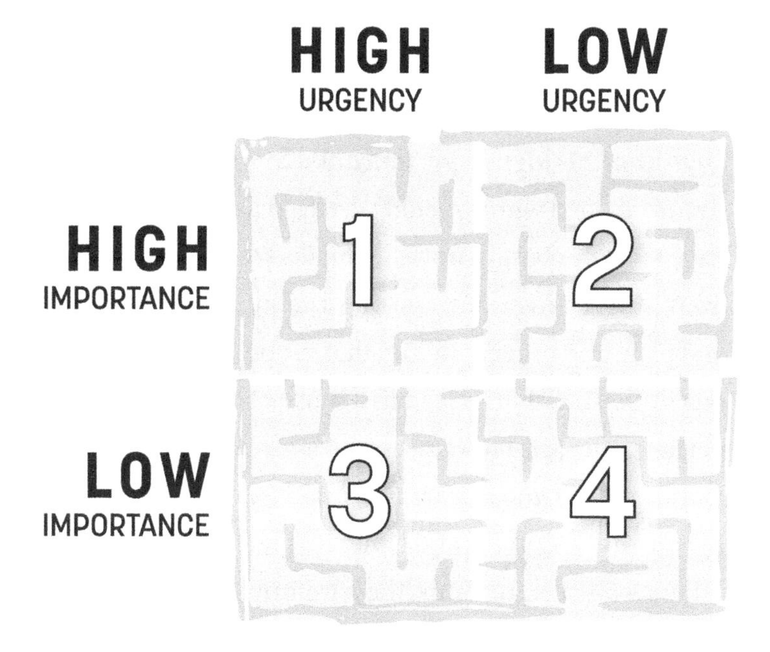

Using this time management quadrant tool, I now could look at everything I was doing and assess where I spent my time, quadrant by quadrant. Important activities are those that help me achieve my high-priority goals whereas urgent activities relate to getting things done now, addressing tasks that are in my immediate vicinity, or maybe doing something that someone else wants me to do.

I now had a tool to objectively see where I'd been spending most of my time. Plus, I could assess how effective and beneficial my actions had been. Let me explain each of the quadrants and illustrate them with real-life examples.

- ***Quadrant 1 is high importance and high urgency.*** These activities are a response to significant problems or a crisis. For instance, finding out a loved one is on the way to the emergency room, realizing an unfinished deadline-driven project is due very soon, or driving a car with the gas tank dial below E for empty and needing to immediately find a gas station. These activities lead to stress, anxiety, and burnout.
- ***Quadrant 2 is high importance and low urgency.*** These activities are aligned with your long-term goals and values but do not have to be done right now. Examples are continuous learning, exercising, eating right, creating a company's long-term vision and plan, and other activities that support your business or life goals. These activities lead to a sense of control, balance, high performance, and fewer crises.
- ***Quadrant 3 is low importance and high urgency.*** These activities are interruptions and issues that may look important (and others want you to think they are important), but in reality, they are not important at all. For instance, most phone calls, emails, and texts; a coworker stopping by the office to chat about last night's ballgame; or a social media banner on the cellphone that grabs your attention. These activities lead to staying busy and maybe even being more popular, but they do not result in achieving your important goals. Spending time in Quadrant 3 is often a sign of a lack of discipline, because the

focus is on short-term tasks rather than long-term goals. This results in wasting time, accomplishing little, and even feeling like a victim when you "don't have time" to finish projects by their due date or achieve important goals.

- ***The last, Quadrant 4, is low in importance and low in urgency.*** These activities basically include doing too much of anything. Examples are binge-watching TV, playing nonstop video games, gossiping, or sleeping in way too late. These activities lead to a lack of responsibility, flakiness, or maybe even getting fired.

Looking at some of my past behaviors helped me see which quadrant my actions fell into. For instance, when Jim, our lone maintenance man, turned in his resignation, I was worried I could not find anyone in town who had experience with our kind of industrial equipment. Even if I could find a maintenance person, reading the manufacturers' manuals would not work well due to all the changes that had been made to our machines over the years. I did not know the details of the machines either, so if Jim had left, no one could keep the aging machines running for our laundry. We wouldn't have been able to deliver services to our customers. You bet this was important to me! And since Jim was about to leave at the end of the week, the situation was urgent too. So fixing this issue was clearly a Quadrant 1 activity (high importance, high urgency).

Looking at certain activities through this lens gave me so much insight! In another example, when I started college at Nyenrode in the Netherlands, all students had to live on campus, and I immediately loved my new freedom that came with being away from home. Our dormitory room housed three students with a bed and desk for each of us. Like me, one of my roommates, Mike, was into card games. We arranged a table and chairs in the middle of our room and invited neighbors to join us. Soon we spent entire days playing Kings and skipping classes. College was a lot of fun this way, and I quickly became popular with my neighbors for providing a place to hang out and play cards. However, playing cards skillfully ranked pretty darn low in importance on achieving my life goals.

When friends would come to my dormitory room and ask if we could play cards for an hour, it became an "urgent" activity. It was something to do right now, in my immediate vicinity, and others wanted me to do it, therefore, making this activity high in urgency. Clearly, this was an example of a Quadrant 3 activity (low importance, high urgency).

Then, when we continued playing cards after that initial hour and ended up playing from noon until midnight, the activity became quite excessive with low importance and low urgency. This marathon card playing was an example of a Quadrant 4 activity (low importance, low urgency).

At Nyenrode Business University, our year was divided into three equal parts made up of ten weeks of classes, one week off, and then one week of exams. Throughout the first ten weeks of each trimester I would make it to a few classes to get to know the professor and find some fellow students who were good at taking notes. At the end of the ten weeks, I made sure I was close enough to one of the regular students, so he would let me borrow his notes to review. I would then spend a small fortune in quarters at the Xerox machine copying his notes.

During the study week of each trimester, I hurried home with all my books and freshly copied notes, and I would start cramming nonstop. I studied from early in the morning until late at night every day. I was counting on my ability to stay focused for long periods of time to cram all this work into one week. Nothing and nobody would get me away from my desk. Passing my exams and finishing college was very important to me and a high-priority goal. Since the exams were held the next week, this activity was high in urgency too. That means studying hard during that week was a Quadrant 1 activity (high importance, high urgency). This example shows how a Quadrant 1 activity can lead to stress, anxiety, and burnout.

Of course, at the time I was just cramming and passing exams rather than learning. Going to classes every day and doing my homework assignments on time would have been the only way to remember and truly learn for my future. Choosing to act more responsibly and proactively would have been a Quadrant 2 activity (high importance, low urgency). It would have been important, because studying regularly would have supported my high-priority goal of finishing college and truly learning about business. It would have been low urgency, because I would have chosen to do my studying well before the deadline of the exam.

Looking back, another example comes to mind. Preparing for my Opa and Oma's anniversary speech months in advance was of high importance to achieve my high-priority goal of not going through the rest of my life stuttering. Since I had several months to prepare and practice for this speech, the activity was low in urgency. So this was another example of a Quadrant 2 activity (high importance, low urgency).

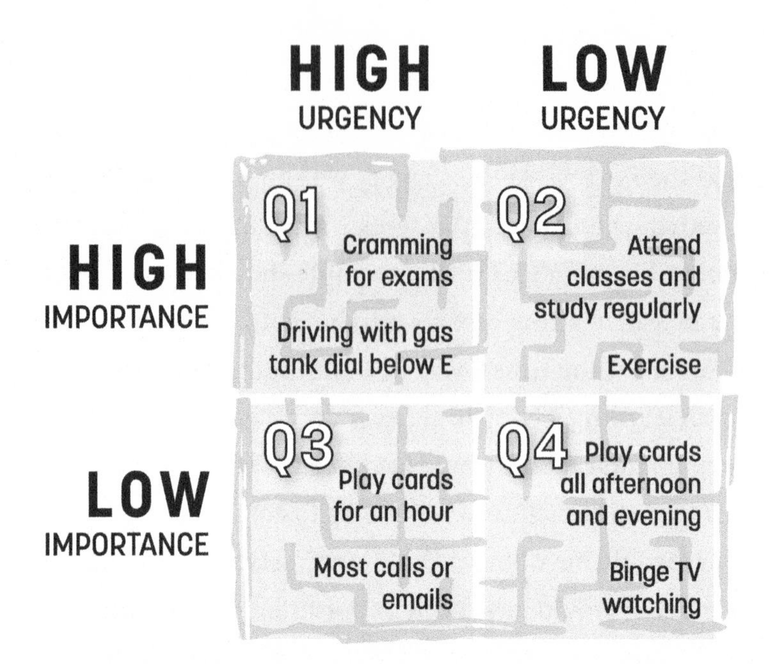

At the time I began thinking about these life examples — and their respective quadrants — I was incredibly busy, overwhelmed, and consumed with crossing items off my endless task list. As I pondered these examples, it was interesting to see when and under what circumstances I "lived in" the four quadrants. I realized that it was possible to begin acting in a more conscious manner. In order to free up more time immediately — and to know I was spending my time on the right activities — I had to take three steps:

1. First, I needed to create the habit of pausing and assessing each activity before I took any action.
2. The next step was to learn to place each activity in its appropriate quadrant.

3. The third and last step was the most critical. To apply these new insights I asked myself questions such as: Is this the most important activity to be doing right now? Should I be doing this at all?

In order to create my new habit, I set my timer for sixty minutes and, when the alarm went off, I briefly stopped what I was doing to consider how I'd spent my time in the previous sixty minutes. In addition to asking myself the above questions, I considered the following:

- In which quadrant did I initially place my activity?
- In which quadrant did it really belong?
- If my activity initially fell into a quadrant other than where it belonged, why did I first put it in the wrong quadrant?

Within just a few days my new habit of assessing every issue first and assigning the issue to the correct quadrant began to form. This became my new way of looking at my world. I remember in the beginning how embarrassed I felt about all the time I had been wasting. Quickly that humiliation turned into excitement when I started to realize the opportunities to free up my time to work on issues that were most important to me.

I also learned that Quadrant 4 (low importance, low urgency) is low-hanging fruit and easy picking. Once I saw the activities that belonged in Quadrant 4, I was able to quickly stop those activities and save that time.

For instance, soon after moving to Searcy, Arkansas, I was asked to help coach a high-school age soccer team. I enjoyed helping these kids and liked sharing my soccer skills, but coaching other kids while ignoring my own family was not in line with my long-term goals. Therefore, I quickly stopped coaching this team.

It's also helpful to remember that Quadrant 1 activities (high importance, high urgency) will always be there. Things happen in life, and there is much over which we have no control. The key insight for me was to focus not on eliminating — but on reducing — the total number of Quadrant 1 crises. I began to see that everything ignored in Quadrant 2 (high importance, low urgency) will eventually move over to Quadrant 1!

Keep in mind that while Quadrant 2 issues are not urgent, they are important, so chances are they will not go away by themselves. An issue just becomes more urgent over time until it's ultimately another full-blown crisis!

For example, if I don't eat and drink healthily long enough (think pizza and beer), my body will eventually revolt, and I'll end up in the emergency room. I started to identify past Quadrant 1 crises I had created myself by procrastinating — and tried to learn from them. What could I change in my behaviors now in order to avoid repeating these self-created Quadrant 1 crises in my future? It took a while, but this deliberate change in my behavior did result in fewer Quadrant 1 crises and more freed up time for me.

By far my biggest time savings came from moving out of Quadrant 3 (low importance, high urgency) and investing that time into Quadrant 2 activities (high importance, low urgency). This was also the hardest transition to make. Quadrant 3 tasks (low importance, high urgency) can feel and act like Quadrant 1 activities (high importance, high urgency), because they appeared to have the same level of urgency. However, I realized that my past Quadrant 3 activities were often based on the priorities of others, seemed fun or popular, or made me feel productive, since I could check something off my list. But just because I wanted to work on a task, that does not mean it is high in importance. (Remember my example of college friends coming to my room to play cards for "just an hour." I dropped whatever I was doing to meet their request. That example illustrates high urgency as well as low importance.)

I remember how, in the early days of our company, managers would line up outside my office to get an answer from me. Or I would, have an issue or question and walk into their office and interrupt whatever they were doing. This "urgency" pushed a lot of our activities into hectic, disruptive, and stress-producing Quadrant 3 activities that impacted productivity, but it didn't need to be that way.

The solution was to set up a weekly one-on-one meeting for up to one hour with each manager. I would place any questions I had for a manager throughout the week in that manager's file to discuss a few days later. Knowing we had a one-on-one, prescheduled hour soon dramatically reduced our Quadrant 3 interruptions with each other.

Once I learned to put many of these high-urgency, low-importance activities correctly in Quadrant 3, saying NO to them became a lot easier, resulting in much more free time. This newfound free time allowed me to work on my Quadrant 2 activities (high importance, low urgency). The more I worked in Quadrant 2, the fewer Quadrant 1 (high importance, high urgency) crises I had in my life. With all this extra time invested in my Quadrant 2 activities, I began to feel my life was much more under control and in balance.

One of my favorite sayings from author Jim Collins is, "Good is the enemy of great." I discovered that the "bad" stuff of Quadrant 4 was easy to spot and eliminate. It was much harder to detect what feels like "good" stuff in Quadrant 3 and stop those activities in order to make room for the "great" stuff of Quadrant 2.

What helped me at this phase in my journey was to realize that each time I said YES to a low-importance Quadrant 3 activity, I was essentially saying NO to one of my high-importance Quadrant 2 activities, which prevented me from doing "great" work. With that awareness, I began to focus more time and energy on Quadrant 2 activities. In time my "good" work did, in fact, become "great" work!

Now that I was feeling less overwhelmed and more in control, I broadened my thinking. What could I do immediately to live more in alignment with all that was important to me — and live in alignment with my values? Obviously, our kids would certainly make it on any list of what I value most in my life and were indeed so dear to me I would risk my life to protect them. What could I do now to show them how important they are to me?

The neighborhood school bus stop was right in front of our house, and every morning around 7:30 the bus would pick up all the kids. School started at 8:00 am. One morning Kathy had to be at the company early, and I was waiting for the school bus with all the neighborhood kids when a realization hit me. A few months before that, I had started meeting with key customers over breakfast rather than having a lunch meeting. The customers canceled less often, there were fewer phone call interruptions, the customer was less distracted, and breakfast was cheaper than lunch!

Well, I thought, if my children were more important to me than even my largest customer, what about a one-on-one breakfast date with each of them? So every week I started sitting down with one of our kids to pick a morning that week for breakfast. If I had a meeting with a large customer, I would not change that appointment unless there was a major emergency, and I treated this child's breakfast with the same significance. Once a week at 7:00 a.m. I would leave our house with one of our kids (who was in charge of selecting the local restaurant for breakfast), and I tried really hard to just listen to whatever topic they wanted to talk about. I would have them at school by 8:00 a.m. and drive on to work.

This one-on-one hour each week with no interruptions and no agenda became very special for all of us, and it lasted many years. If I had not gone through the exercise of asking myself what was truly important to me, I would have never even thought of this weekly one-on-one breakfast hour with each of our kids. That breakfast hour with just one child felt so right, it grew into a cherished weekly tradition. It very much felt like moving from a "good" hour at work to a "great" hour with one of our kids.

I invite you to start applying what you just learned right away. In the next chapter you will find exercises and worksheets to apply the four quadrants in your professional and personal life. You will soon start to see your world in a new way. You can then use this new freed-up time to work on your Quadrant 2 activities (high importance, low urgency), which will help you connect your present activities to your future goals. As we'll discuss later, this is a critical step in Creating Your Best You.

EXERCISE

List examples in your past in which you were "living in" each of the four quadrants. Explain why each example belongs in its particular quadrant and what, if anything, you would do differently.

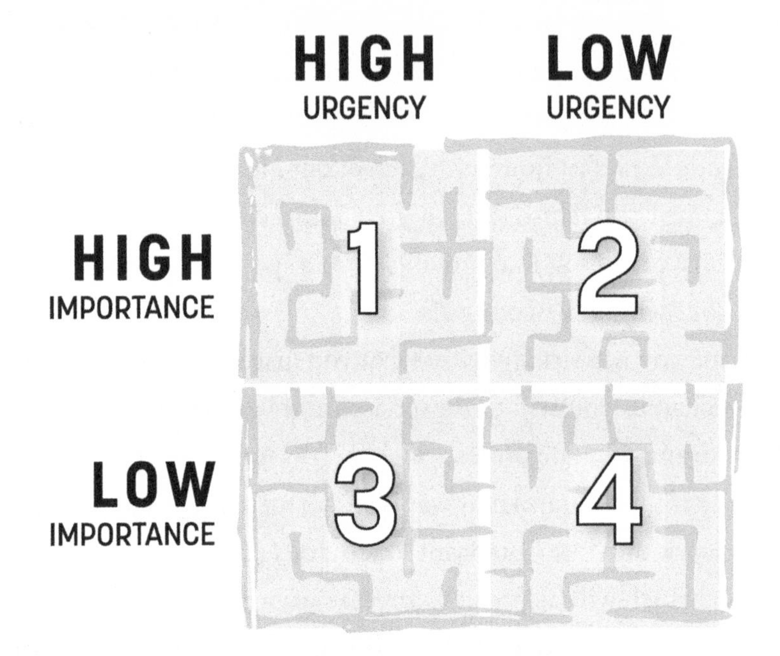

Quadrant 1 (high importance, high urgency)

____

____

____

Quadrant 2 (high importance, low urgency)

____

____

____

Quadrant 3 (low importance, high urgency)

____

____

____

Quadrant 4 (low importance, low urgency)

____

____

____

CHAPTER 8

USING THE TIME MANAGEMENT QUADRANT TOOL IN YOUR LIFE

HOW CAN YOU PRACTICE USING this time management quadrant tool in your personal and professional life? Here's more detail on what worked for me when I was practicing this new skill: I set the timer on my cellphone for one hour for virtually every task or activity in both my professional and personal life. I also carried a single sheet of paper everywhere I went. On one side were the following nine questions and on the other side was a blank copy of the daily Working with Quadrants worksheet that I created. After the timer went off, I would take a few minutes to reflect on these nine questions:

1. Did I pause before I jumped into the activity?
2. Did I give the activity a quadrant number?

3. Was my initial quadrant assignment correct even after deeper reflection now?

4. If not, why did it change?

5. Once I assigned a quadrant, did I follow through with correct behavior?

6. Did I stop doing a Quadrant 4 activity?

7. Did I find a Quadrant 3 task "disguised" as Quadrant 1 and then stop doing that activity?

8. Did I find more time for Quadrant 2 work?

9. What else can I change in my environment or routines to create more Quadrant 2 time?

As I reflected on that hour's activity, I made a quick note to describe the activity, honestly assign the appropriate quadrant, and jot down what I learned on my daily worksheet. Included here is a detailed example of one of my daily Working with Quadrants worksheets.

EXAMPLE WORKSHEET

Working with Quadrants

Day: *Tuesday*
Q1 high importance, high urgency
Q2 high importance, low urgency
Q3 low importance, high urgency
Q4 low importance, low urgency

5:00 a.m.	NordicTrack exercise. Reading *Speed of Trust* (Q2).
6:00	Cool down and stretch (Q2), shower/shave (Q2), breakfast with kids (Q2), drive to work (Q2).
7:00	Talk 20 minutes at coffee station about last night's game with Mike (Q3). Review minutes of leadership meeting (Q1).
8:00	Leadership meeting (Q1).
9:00	Type minutes right after meeting of who does what by when (Q2). Return call to industry friend (Q3 mostly).
10:00	15-minutes reading news (Q3). Cleaned out inbox 15 minutes (mostly Q3). 30-minute weekly meeting with sales manager (Q2).
11:00	45-minute weekly meeting with service manager (Q2). 15-minute talk in lunchroom with Jack (Q3).
12:00 p.m.	Lunch at Main Street Café with production manager as weekly meeting (Q2).
1:00	Answer emails, 4 phone calls, 3 interruptions into office (almost all Q3).
2:00	Telling service manager how to handle customer rather

	than letting him decide and learn (Q3).
3:00	Plant tour and visit with production workers, office, and route drivers. Ask about their family and ask, "If you had a magic wand and could change one thing we are doing, what would that one thing be?" (Q2).
4:00	Talk 20 minutes to Bob in hallway. Mostly me talking (Q3). Clean out papers from inbox (Q3).
5:00	Emails, phone calls, social media (Q3). Plan for tomorrow (Q2). Return home.
6:00	Dinner with Kathy and kids and hear about their day (Q2). Give kids bath and ready for bed (Q2).
7:00	Read to kids (Q2).
8:00	Watch TV to relax (Q2).
9:00	And then watch more TV (Q4).
10:00	To bed for 7 to 8 hours of sleep (Q2).

YOUR WORKSHEET

Actively managing your time to allow room for more Quadrant 2 activities is important for both your professional and personal life. This is a critical step in the process of Creating Your Best You. To begin, download this form from our website (www.CreatingYBY.com) and make seven copies of this worksheet. You will complete one worksheet every day for the next seven days. As you move through your day, hour by hour, make a brief note to describe that hour's activity and assign it to an appropriate quadrant. Be as objective as possible! At the end of the week, spend a few minutes reviewing your worksheets. Most likely, your honest assessments will reveal surprising trends — and helpful insights.

Working with Quadrants

Day: _____

Q1 high importance, high urgency

Q2 high importance, low urgency

Q3 low importance, high urgency

Q4 low importance, low urgency

5:00 a.m. ______________________________

6:00 ______________________________

7:00 ______________________________

8:00 ______________________________

9:00 ______________________________

10:00 ______________________________

11:00 ______________________________

12:00 p.m. ______________________________

1:00 ______________________________

2:00 ______________________________

3:00 ______________________________

4:00 ______________________________

5:00 ______________________________

6:00 ______________________________

7:00 ______________________________

8:00 ______________________________

9:00 ______________________________

10:00 ______________________________

As a result of this quadrant work, chances are you will be able to allocate more time to important activities in your life. Although this is a "good" step in the right direction, to maximize your benefits of this quadrant work and make a "great" leap forward you need to get true clarity on what is important to you. What do you value above all else? What are your high-priority, long-term goals?

Once you are clear about your values, you can much more easily and accurately assign a high or low importance rating to your many activities. In the next chapter, we will begin to discover and clarify what is truly important to you, a major component of Creating Your Best You.

CHAPTER 9

DEFINING WHAT IS IMPORTANT AND IDENTIFYING YOUR CORE VALUES

VALUES ARE OUR JUDGMENT of what is important in our life and influence our highest priorities over an extended period. Values are different and very personal for each individual and are based on our unique combination of experiences, beliefs, and evaluations. Our values have a major influence on our preferences and choices, our motivation, and objectives as well as our moral principles and our character.

To be clear, values are different than goals. Our values determine what we think is important, whereas a goal is something we want to achieve. For me, the key learning around values and goals was that I could get satisfaction either from doing what I value or from achieving goals. However, when I focused on achieving goals that were aligned with my values, I experienced a much deeper and greater happiness.

Identifying my values was more of a discovery process than a selection process. My values were already in my thoughts, behaviors, and priorities, but they were floating around in my head and comfortably vague, allowing me convenient "wiggle room" for some inconsistent behaviors.

Getting my top values out of my head and written down in front of me forced me to think through what I truly found was important and what was, ultimately, less important. The clarity that came with knowing and living up to my core values helped me to make better decisions in both my professional and personal life when I came to those moments of truth — times when I had to make a difficult choice at a critical fork in the road.

This need for clarity about why it's important to live in alignment with my values *before* I'm in the heat of the battle was driven home to me while watching a videotape I had recorded. Our son, Adam, was about seven years old and played on a local youth soccer team with a handful of other boys. As coach, I decided to use my new video camera and tripod to record the game. I set it up on the side of the field behind the bench for our extra players. I had pushed "record," and the tape ran by itself for the next hour.

At the time, soccer was still a new sport in rural Arkansas, and the league officials emphasized that the primary goal was for the children to have fun while chasing the soccer ball. On that day we played the one other team that was about as talented as ours. As coach I really wanted us to win and take the lead in the standings. I knew we played soccer to have a good time, but I was also convinced it was easier to have fun when you win!

Well, we ended up losing a close game, and I was not happy. A few days later when I was over my grumpy mood and before our next practice, I wanted to see what the team should focus on next. As I played the videotape back on the TV in our family room, I remember wishing I could hide behind the couch. I was so embarrassed by my behavior! In the video, I was yelling at the kids nonstop and telling them what to do. I was yelling the most at our son, Adam. I micromanaged every move he made. Even when he did what I told him to do — and if it did not work out — I blamed Adam as if it were somehow his fault!

I wanted to win that game and that had somehow become more important than being a positive coach and parent. Wow, did I ever fail my moment of truth and pick the wrong path at that fork in the road! I was ashamed and mortified when showing the video to Kathy. Who is this guy screaming at the kids? It was amazing that Adam was still playing soccer at all!

After that humbling experience I saw the light and knew I needed to get very clear on my values as soccer coach *before* I got in the middle of a close game. The coach I wanted to become was all about the kids learning soccer skills, having fun, experiencing true teamwork, and ultimately using soccer to build their self-esteem. This soccer coaching experience was an embarrassing wakeup call for me. It was time to get clear on what was truly important in my life and to make sure my activities and attitudes aligned with those core values.

The way I initially clarified my values was to just sit down quietly, think through and write down my values, and then put them in priority order. This worked well, and I can say now while looking back over the last thirty years that my list of core values has not fundamentally changed. I now use prettier phrases, but the meaning and order are essentially the same as when I started this process. Although sitting down in silence with a piece of paper worked well as a first go-around, I want to share with you two exercises that helped me to further clarify my values.

EXERCISE

Accountability
Achievement
Advancement
Adventure
Aesthetic
Appearance
Art
Authenticity
Authority
Balance
Belonging
Camaraderie
Challenge
Commitment
Communication
Community
Compassion
Competence
Competition
Connection
Consensus
Contribution
Courage
Health
Honesty
Honor
Humility
Independence
Inner harmony
Integrity
Intellectual status
Knowledge
Learning
Love
Loyalty
Morality
Music
Neatness
Openness
Patriotism
Peace
Perseverance
Personal growth
Play
Pleasure
Power
Professionalism
Prosperity
Rationality
Recognition
Relationships
Religion
Respect
Responsibility
Security
Self-acceptance
Self-control
Service
Spirituality
Stability
Success
Support
Teamwork
Tolerance
Tradition
Travel
Trust
Understanding
Vitality
Wealth
Wellness
Winning
Wisdom

The first exercise to help clarify your values starts with this list of possible values (other values can be added as needed). Circle all the values that apply to you, or download the list at www.CreatingYBY.com As you circle the values on the list, keep the following questions in mind:

- What are my highest priorities in life?
- What do I treasure?
- What makes me feel glad to be alive?

If you circled a lot of words, here's a way to distill your list to just a few core values. When I looked at all my circled values I took a minute to create groups of similar values. I picked the most representative value for the group or found a new descriptive word for that group. Lastly, I prioritized my list several times until I had my list of values down to a handful of the most important ones to me: my core values.

For instance, I had circled values such as balance, connection, inner harmony, health, play, religion, spirituality, vitality, and wellness. After thinking through the deeper meaning for each word I had circled, I ultimately grouped that set of values as *Health*. It fit well when I chose to define *Health* as including all four dimensions of our human nature — not only physical health but also mental, social, and spiritual health.

Once I had the correct word to describe my first core value, I added a short, one-sentence explanation of the deeper Why and what I meant to accomplish by this core value. For *Health* my intention was to work on the physical, mental, social, and spiritual sides of my life in order to keep doing fun activities and stay relevant for as long as possible to the ones I love. I felt a deep motivation around this value when picturing spending quality time with my kids and grandkids far into my future.

This value of *Health* was all about maintaining and improving the quality of my physical, mental, social, and spiritual life to become older gracefully. My one-sentence description of my Why and What for this core value became: *Health: to live younger, longer*. List the values you circled below.

____

____

____

____

____

____

____

____

____

____

____

____

EXERCISE

Another exercise that helped me clarify my values is called *Determine Your Values: Step by Step* by Gulnar Vaswani. This process starts from your daily life and then works backward to help you identify your core values. I encourage you to complete this exercise as well to determine your core values:

Step one: Answer the following thirteen questions with three answers for each question:

1. How do you fill your personal space?
2. How do you spend your time?
3. How do you spend your energy and what energizes you?
4. How do you spend your money?
5. Where are you most organized?
6. Where are you most reliable?
7. What dominates your thoughts on how you want to live your life?
8. What do you visualize most?
9. What do you most often talk to yourself about?
10. What do you most often talk to others about?
11. What inspires you?
12. What goals stand out in your life and have stood the test of time?
13. What do you love to learn or read about the most?

Step two: Identify the answers that repeat most often.

Out of the thirteen questions multiplied by three answers each, you will come up with thirty-nine answers. Now look for repetition among your answers. Watch for the same value being expressed in different ways. For example, "spending time with people I like," "having a drink with the folks from work," and "going out to eat with my friends" are all the same value. Look at the answer that is most often repeated and write beside it the number of times it repeats. Then find the second most frequent answer, then the third, and so on until you have ranked every single answer. This list gives you a good primary indicator of how your life is already demonstrating your commitment to these values.

Step three: Reflect, evaluate, and prioritize the list to determine your handful of core values. Ideally, you'll arrive at just a few core values — identifying three core values is a great goal.

How can you trim your list of core values? Insights from my discovery process may be helpful

Did you find any recurring themes in your answers? Were you able to pinpoint your core values? Relating my experience may be helpful as you consider and refine your core values. When I looked at my thirty-nine answers to the thirteen questions, I quickly saw a dominant theme. I found one of my three answers to almost every question related to my immediate family, extended family, or friends. After reflecting on what each answer really meant, I combined all these values into one core value: *Relationships.*

After nailing down the one right word to describe this second core value, I wanted to add the one-sentence explanation of Why and What my intentions are for this core value. While working on describing *Relationships,* I immediately struggled. My initial challenge was which role came first: to be a loving father or a wonderful husband? I love our three kids, and as a father I could make a difference in how they grew up and who they became. In the end, I started to see that the best thing I could do for our kids was to model being a good husband and being in a loving relationship with Kathy. So after being a husband came my role as father, then grandfather, then my role in my relationships with my extended family and friends. The core value and the short description of the purpose and intention became: *Relationships: Highest priority on my key relationships — wife, kids, grandkids, family, and friends.*

Other words that kept showing up for me as important values were achievement, competition, challenge, competence, integrity, learning, loyalty, perseverance, personal growth, productivity, success, trust, and teamwork. It took several years and many rounds of writing, thinking, and rewriting before I ultimately found a way to describe these values in my third and last core value: *My best self.*

This principle has shown up as a high priority in my activities for a long time. It shows up in the way I have always sought out new opportunities and challenges to improve myself. Whether it was to commit to give that speech at Opa and Oma's party as a teenager, or to emigrate to the U.S. when I was twenty-one, or to start our own company seven years later. I felt genuine delight in continuously improving our small company and worked hard to keep one step ahead as our fast-growing company entered into its next level of the corporate life cycle.

I just love believing I can be a bit better tomorrow than I am today. A few years after we sold the company and stopped working, several friends told me I was just too old to learn to play golf decently, since I had never played before. During the first few years, every time we played a round of golf, they would beat me by at least thirty strokes.

After many lessons with our local country club pro and lots of hours of practice, my golf scores came down a lot. When playing with those same friends, I now beat them by ten strokes! Few things motivate me more than hearing it just cannot be done! In short, I love the challenge, the learning, the feedback, and getting better over time.

Being all in, trying as hard as I can, and absolutely believing I can be a bit better tomorrow than I am today has been a core value of mine for as long as I can remember. As I was trying to think through where this all came from and how long I have been acting like this, I went back to my childhood. What I remember around this value dates back to my first report card in elementary school at Saint Bavo School in the Netherlands. Our semester report cards showed subjects such as Math, Writing, Reading, and a few more. However, on the very top of the report card were Diligence and Zeal, Conduct, and Neatness.

When I got a report card, my parents almost exclusively focused on those three categories at the top of the list. They only glanced at the grades for Math, Writing, Reading, and so forth, since they believed good grades in these classes reflected natural intelligence and talents.

In their view, intelligence and other talents were just a gift at birth based on one's parents' DNA and their environment. However, *how* I used my intelligence and talents was totally up to me, under my control, and absolutely my responsibility. Over the years, I saw that they really lived those values consistently, and they taught me that anything short of an A grade on Diligence and Zeal, Conduct, and Neatness was totally unacceptable and all on me! Perhaps this story explains to some extent my intensity levels and perseverance as well as my need to make the most of what I have been given in order to become better tomorrow. Defining my third core value's Why and What in one sentence, became: *My best self: To continuously improve and to give it all I have.*

In this chapter, I have shown you several exercises I used to discover my core values and how I described and touched on my underlying motivations for each of my core values. Once I was clear on my core values, I now knew what was truly important to me. (If you have not yet completed those two exercises, I encourage you to do so now.)

In addition, when using the time management quadrant tool to evaluate and prioritize all my activities, I now had the confidence to accurately assign a high or low importance by evaluating the activity's impact on my core values. I now knew in which of the four quadrants any activity truly belonged!

I enjoyed the progress I had made so far, yet I knew I could still be clearer. The next step was to further translate my core values and motivations into straightforward, easy-to-understand daily activities. How could I state so clearly what living in alignment with my core values looked like that when I reflected on my behaviors, I had no "wiggle room" left? In the next chapter, I will show you the process I used to answer this important question to create further clarity in my life.

CHAPTER 10

MOVING FROM CORE VALUES TO DAILY BEHAVIORS

LET ME SUMMARIZE at a high level how I began the process of developing my life masterplan. I started out sharing how unsustainable my life was and how my body revolted. I was overwhelmed and confused with all the daily activities I felt I had to complete, and yet I felt guilty about the stuff I did not do. And really, how intentional and present was I with the activities I did do?

Rather than reshuffling my to-do list constantly, I discovered a new tool — the time management quadrant tool — to help me properly prioritize my life's activities. As I shared in a previous chapter, I would take each activity and assign it a high or low rating to importance and urgency and then place each activity in one of four quadrants. Knowing what was urgent was fairly easy to figure out since it is, by definition, immediate and in my face. Much harder was deciding what was truly important to me. To discover what was genuinely important to me I worked through several exercises and spelled out my core values — each with a brief explanation.

Now it was time to take the next logical step. I realized I needed to find the answers to these questions:

- What do each of my core values mean in my day-to-day life?
- How would I know if I actually am living these values — or not?
- How could I create that deep, satisfied feeling of achieving goals that are aligned with my core values?
- How could I get results in areas that matter to me while holding myself accountable — without wiggle room?

It was time to carefully convert each core value into specific daily behaviors and attitudes. In the following chapters, I'll share my process and learnings as well as guidance and exercises for you to discover answers to these same questions.

CHAPTER 11

DAILY BEHAVIORS FOR YOUR FIRST CORE VALUE

I TACKLED MY CORE VALUE of *Relationships: highest priority on my key relationships — wife, kids, grandkids, family, and friends* first. What would my daily behaviors and attitudes look like? What was I doing that was incongruent with this core value?

When I visualized how I wanted to be versus how I actually behaved in my key relationships, the first thing I could immediately work on was being more present. Multitasking always made me feel productive and efficient. For example, I read business books while working out on the NordicTrack every morning. I just loved doing two tasks in the timeframe of one. While multitasking might work with some duties, I now see I mostly overrated it. Multitasking could easily result in not doing either task well. Xunzi, a Chinese philosopher living around 312 B.C. said it well: "The person attempting to travel two roads at once will get nowhere."

When it comes to people and relationships, I realized multitasking could easily be downright inefficient and actually counterproductive. Giving people my full attention without any distractions created a feeling of support and care. This certainly was the case when I started to turn off all distractions during my weekly hourlong meeting with each key leadership team member. I needed to bring that same attitude and behavior from my business into my key personal relationships.

Being present, supportive, and showing I genuinely cared was a good start to translate my core value around *Relationships* into my daily behaviors. However, there was more ground to cover. What I defined so far was my behavior when I was with someone. Today, our kids are spread across the U.S. What was my envisioned behavior with family members who lived somewhere else in this vast country? Together with our three kids, Kathy and I now cover all four continental time zones. How do we stay connected and close to each other while living so far apart?

Remember my Opa and Oma for whom I gave that scary first public speech? Well, they were a genuine example of how to live family values. Although they had done well financially, Opa and Oma lived their whole married life modestly in the same row house on the outskirts of The Hague. What was important to them was to use their savings for large family gatherings to keep everyone connected. At least once a year Opa and Oma found some excuse to give a huge family-wide party for their twelve children and all the grandkids and great-grandkids. For particularly special occasions, the family parties were hosted at a fancy hotel in Luxembourg for a long weekend.

As my grandparents got older, they came up with a creative way to perpetuate this important family value. They gifted me and every other grandchild 1,000 euros a year and "requested" that half of this amount, 500 euros, would be voluntarily donated into a trust fund to finance these family gatherings after they had passed on. Quickly we learned that grandkids who kept all 1,000 euros indeed could keep that money but did not receive any money the following year! Soon everyone donated half of their gift to the trust. Today that trust still finances an annual Giezeman day, bringing almost everyone in the family together twenty years after Opa and Oma passed away.

During his final year Opa paid for and was the driving force to publish a *Giezeman Book*. In this book each family member had their own page with a photo, basic information, personal interests, favorite saying, and future expectations as well as his or her place in the family tree. Every handful of years this *Giezeman Book* gets updated and republished and serves as another way to keep the family connected. Recently, the sixth edition of the fully updated *Giezeman Book* was published — taking on the heft of a small phone book. What clarity Opa and Oma had on how important family was in their lives and what a legacy to leave!

One example of how I put staying connected into practice started about twenty-five years ago. Kathy suggested I call my parents in the Netherlands every Sunday rather than haphazardly. Calling every week around the same time has become a wonderful tradition and has helped me to stay close and connected to my parents over the years even though we are so far apart.

Likewise, in my efforts to keep our family connected, I started to work on getting all our children and lately, grandchildren, together for a weeklong vacation. Jobs, limited vacation time, the challenge of raising little children, and the struggle to find a location we all liked made it difficult. In discussing the idea, it also became clear that if our married kids spend a week with us, they also wanted to spend similar time with the other parents. Once that hesitant feeling was out in the open, we could easily adapt our plan. We could rent a bigger house and invite the in-laws too! We ended up with a wonderful week together. Every couple was in charge of one dinner, shared babysitting duties, and the married children were able to enjoy time with both sets of parents.

I believe this event would not have happened if I had not clarified my core value into what exactly that meant for my day-to-day behavior. Achieving this goal of a vacation week with the whole family together was directly aligned with this core value and felt so wonderful!

After several reflections and re-writings, I now describe my daily behaviors and attitudes around relationships as *Relationships: Highest priority on my key relationships: Wife, kids, grandkids, family, and friends. I am present, supportive, and genuinely caring. I constantly look for new opportunities for us to connect and follow up accordingly.*

EXERCISE

Write down your first core value. Now spend a few minutes thinking about how various daily behaviors and attitudes could support that core value. Try to distill your thoughts into one or two sentences that guide you to identify specific, ongoing daily behaviors and attitudes that support your first core value. Take your time and think deeply. You are laying the foundation to ensure your present activities move you ever-closer to your future goals!

CHAPTER 12

DAILY BEHAVIORS FOR YOUR SECOND CORE VALUE

NEXT CAME MY CORE VALUE AROUND my health. What specific behaviors did I need to spell out to clarify my vision for *Health: To live younger, longer.* What did I need to define, so there was no "wiggle room" left — and at the end of the week I could say "yes, I did that" or "no, I did not do that"?

Right after that health scare with my migraine, Doctor Dan convinced me that my ten-year goal should be going into my forties in great shape. It is much more difficult to get back in shape as you get older. He also drove home the point of doing annual health exams for the sake of my own family as well as all the families depending on me to stay healthy and keep the company alive and growing.

With regard to health, I learned much from my dad — unfortunately. He was loving and caring and worked hard. He was not particularly athletic; the two "sports" he played were bridge and chess. Most of my childhood we lived next door to my parents' family business, a hospital linen supply laundry. Dad was at work firing up the boiler before 6:00 every morning and took no time for breakfast or lunch. He consumed his calories through the sugar and cream in his coffee while smoking two packs of unfiltered Golden Fiction cigarettes each day.

At the end of each shift dad and two other foremen retreated to the company office at the ground floor of our house and discussed the day's events over several Heineken beers. Dad ate a small dinner while consuming a few more beers, took a quick nap on the couch, and had more beer during the evening as our family watched TV. This was his routine throughout his life.

One day when dad was about sixty-five years old, Kathy and I and our three kids flew from Arkansas to the Amsterdam Schiphol Airport for a two-week vacation at my parents' home. Dad was quite emotional, felt weak, and seemed unsure of himself, so mom drove us home from the airport. In the days that followed dad could not remember many things, and every morning when we came downstairs he would say, "Oh, you're here?" A few days later he visited the local hospital for extensive tests.

Ultimately, he was diagnosed with advanced Korsakoff's syndrome due to chronic vitamin B deficiencies, which caused the short-term memory loss. Many years of filling up on beer rather than eating correctly led to this now irreversible illness. Ten year later he passed away from lung cancer, but we had lost him already many years before.

Losing dad too soon and seeing all the special family events he missed served as a huge wakeup call for me. A month after dad was diagnosed with Korsakoff's syndrome I celebrated my birthday, and I decided to stop drinking alcohol for a year until my next birthday — just to make sure I was not an alcoholic. Whatever I wanted to do in my life, if I did not take care of myself, I could not help anyone else. My health is indeed my main asset. It's like putting that airplane emergency oxygen mask on yourself first before you can help others.

Over time, I translated my *Health* core value into the following simple and clear statement: *Health: To live younger, longer. I am intentional about everything I consume, especially alcohol. I stretch, meditate, and exercise at least 5 times per week. I sleep at least 7 hours per night. I have a full physical exam each year. I also schedule weekly activities for my emotional, mental, and spiritual health. I am a "lean, mean golfing machine."*

EXERCISE

Write down your second core value. As with the previous exercise, think about how various daily behaviors and attitudes could support that core value. Take your time as you distill your thoughts into one or two sentences that clarify your daily behaviors and attitudes.

____

____

____

____

____

____

____

____

____

____

____

CHAPTER 13

DAILY BEHAVIORS FOR YOUR THIRD CORE VALUE

LAYING OUT MY DAILY BEHAVIORS around my third and last core value "*My best self: To continuously improve and to give it all I have*" was the most challenging. When I envisioned the best version of myself and looked for gaps with my current behaviors, I quickly concluded I could significantly improve my listening skills. I was definitely guilty of thinking about what I was going to say next rather than genuinely listening. I jokingly have said many times that, "I worked hard on my listening skills, which have improved tremendously over the years, and now they are almost average!"

Learning to listen not only with my ears but also with my eyes and my heart is hard work. I am impatient, often jump to conclusions, and tend to prescribe solutions before accurately diagnosing the issue. At least once a week and often at the end of each day, I would look back and review how well I had listened and what I could have done better.

When I listened well, I was amazed how much people almost instantly showed genuine appreciation and closeness. When it was their turn to listen, they would often return the favor.

I have always felt that the key to my professional and personal success and feeling I was my best self was when I found myself in high-trust situations. When I was in a high-trust relationship, I only needed a half sentence to communicate my thoughts and I could even say something incorrectly — and yet I would still be understood. The conversation would start quickly and work smoothly. Whereas, with low-trust relationships everything slowed down to a crawl, and I needed a lengthy and precise conversation to arrive at an agreement.

I like to define trust as having that feeling of confidence rather than of suspicion when facing the unknown. The reason I was immediately enchanted by *The 7 Seven Habits of Highly Effective People* by Stephen Covey was that this book showed me for the first time *how to do* trust. Sure, like most people I wanted that feeling of high trust, but for the first time I could see a path to get there. The way I could help to create trust was to start working on myself, working from the inside out in my personal and professional relationships. By being able to share who I was, what I wanted, and why that was important to me — and then "walk the talk" — I could more quickly and easily generate integrity and trust.

After studying Covey's book, I took a three-day seminar on applying the Seven Habits to your own life in Little Rock, Arkansas. Over the next six months I focused on implementing the material for myself. I experienced profound improvements in my attitudes and behaviors, and others began to notice changes in me too. As mentioned earlier, we could not afford to send everyone in the company to that three-day seminar, and I decided to become a certified trainer. I taught the seminar in hourlong segments throughout our company. Describing personal examples during our company's classes brought me closer to our teammates, and we now had a common language to use throughout our company.

All this work resulted in higher trust within our leadership team, our frontline teammates, and even our customers. Of course, each time I taught a class, I ended up more fully understanding the material, and I always felt that I had better model what I taught! The material became so ingrained into our company culture that *Inc.* magazine published an in-depth article on how we used Covey's book to create trust in our company.

When I pictured my best self, it was as a highly trusted individual. However, trust is like happiness in the sense that it cannot be created directly. Trust is granted by others, and my role is to help create an environment in which trust can grow. What I can control is to deliberately extend trust and to be consistently trustworthy. I saw two major overall components of developing trustworthiness — competence and character. So how could I specifically spell this out in my daily behaviors and attitudes?

Starting with the first aspect of trustworthiness, how would I become and then stay *competent* as president of a fast-growing company? For me this meant continuing to study business books, attending seminars, visiting colleagues, and learning from consultants. I love to learn, and I embrace changes in my environment as opportunities to get better faster. Being competent also meant I would need to take responsibility to get results and hold myself and others accountable.

What often held me back from achieving many new insights was my nature of being quite competitive, aggressive, and blunt. I enjoy a good verbal challenge and welcome the opposition. Just bring it on! However, other members of the leadership team sometimes just got tired and worn down fighting me on everything. At that time, I had not learned the value of modulating my intensity and showing more respect and humility for other perspectives. The end result was that I missed out on quality feedback and opportunities to learn and improve. Not only would I need to learn to dial back my forcefulness, I would need to encourage feedback and get the untold stories out on the table, so we could deal with the real issues.

At home this was not a problem. Kathy had the strength to conduct the difficult conversations. When I did not get the essence of her message the first time, she would bring out the proverbial two-by-four plank and hit me over the head until I finally heard her. We often jokingly say that we do not have to walk on eggshells in our house! I did not have to look over my shoulder and try to remember what I did wrong two weeks ago — I knew it right then!

At the company I required more help. We worked to improve our leadership teamwork with Bruce Hodes, president and founder of CMI Chicago. He introduced our leadership team to a "caca patrol" process to transform covert conversations into overt ones and to improve mutual trust. At the start of every leadership meeting we would take a few minutes for each member to state out loud a trust score for every other leadership team member. A low score between two people meant those two members had something to work out. Once a low-trust relationship was identified, the two parties had twenty-four hours to set up a one-on-one meeting to clear the air and work through the issue.

Almost always the problem was a miscommunication of sorts or an unintended consequence of some action. In the few instances the two parties could not work it out themselves in a satisfactory way, we would discuss the matter in depth in my office. This process definitely took courage and practice. We immediately lost one leadership team member after instituting this process, but in the end, this exercise got the remaining team members closer and much more trusting of each other. I definitely got more spirited feedback from the executive leaders and better opportunities to improve my competence and learn from my mistakes.

In addition to improving my *competence,* I also needed to work on the second component of trustworthiness: *character*. I wanted to spell out specifically the daily behaviors and attitudes that would be required to develop my character so that trust could grow. What character traits would I need to embrace and model and exactly how should that show up in my behavior? When I thought about character the next word that popped into my mind was integrity. But what specifically did that overused word mean for me? In describing what I meant with integrity for myself I ended up with several statements:

- "I do what I say I will do."
- "I keep my commitments and hold myself accountable."
- For me, integrity also meant a transparency of my intention: "I will clarify expectations, communicate clearly, have no hidden agendas, and show loyalty to others especially when they are not present."

One of the finest examples of integrity I witnessed was when I made the first serious attempt to arrange financing to start our own company. I knew we wanted our own uniform rental business but did not know yet where that business would be. I did know that I had to at least try to build my own company, or I would regret it for the rest of my life. One of my deepest fears was to be sixty-five years old and look back at my career, knowing I never tried to branch out on my own. I would visualize sitting in my rocking chair on my front porch saying: "You are a chickenshit. You lacked the courage to at least take your best shot at running your own company."

Leaving a secure and comfortable career with a large company felt scary at the time but not as scary as calling myself a chickenshit for the rest of my life! Growing up I had frequently heard my dad say that if you want to start your own company, you should do it while you are young. He felt after you are thirty years old you get used to the comforts of a higher income and have the corresponding higher expenses. Well I was twenty-seven and rapidly approaching that mental deadline.

Kathy and I flew to the Netherlands that Christmas to show off our son, Adam. He had been born earlier that year and was the new *stamhouder* (holder of the family tree). It was time to test the waters, and I brought along a dozen copies of the business plan for our imaginary uniform rental company somewhere in the U.S. At a family gathering I invited some family members who owned laundries and whom I perceived as having some financial resources to a presentation. I met with seven potential investors over coffee and pastry at one of their laundries the following Saturday morning. One was my Uncle Wim, one of my dad's younger brothers. He owned several successful hospital laundries in the Netherlands, Germany, England, and one in the U.S. He was aggressive, blunt, intimidating, and enjoyed taking charge.

After my presentation and lots of questions, six members agreed to each invest one-hundred thousand guilders or about thirty-five thousand dollars at that time. Many investors in the room were swayed significantly by Uncle Wim's willingness to invest.

At the end of the meeting Uncle Wim told the others that it was great they wanted to invest their money, but they had to agree this would eventually become Jos and Kathy's company. He stressed that they needed to agree right then and there that when Kathy and I became successful we could buy them out at a fair price. If they were not willing to do so, they should not invest. Uncle Wim said this even though he was to be one of the shareholders. He saw my willingness to give up a lot of ownership and control to make the deal work, and he showed real integrity by protecting me from myself!

Four years after we purchased the company and we were financially stable, we converted all their shares to individual loans at a fifteen percent annual rate of return. Uncle Wim's assistance during that critical initial meeting was a wonderful display of integrity. Uncle Wim showed loyalty to us, even over his own interest as a fellow shareholder. He had no hidden agendas, talked straight, and helped to clarify expectations with the other investors. Our business would have been so much more challenging and less rewarding if we had been financially tied to multiple long-term shareholders.

As I thought about daily behaviors that would support this core value, I realized it was time to sort through all my different thoughts on how I could become my best self. I started by making a comprehensive list including my listening skills, competence enhancing behaviors, character traits, and ways to help create trust. I then used the same process we applied with values where I ranked my most relevant behaviors and traits. After fine-tuning and prioritizing the list several times, I ended up with the few critical traits and behaviors I needed to focus on.

The list of the most important behaviors and character traits to become "*my best self*" ended up with listening well, respect, humility, loyalty, talking straight, extending trust, achievement, and accountability. Once I was satisfied with my list, I went on to describe in detail what each component meant. The book that really spoke to me on this topic was *The Speed of Trust* by Stephen M.R. Covey with Rebecca R. Merrill. Ultimately, I ended up with the following daily behavior statement:

My best self: To continuously improve and to give it all I have. I enjoy being a lifelong learner. I embrace my changing environment. I seek feedback and learn from my mistakes. Specifically, I:

- *Plan weekly — I plan, execute, and evaluate against my priorities weekly. I accept and achieve results in challenging, aligned roles and dare to say a "positive no" to roles that do not resonate.*
- *Demonstrate respect — I show humility. I am fair, kind, open, and civil. I modulate my intensity.*
- *Listen first — I genuinely understand the thoughts and feelings of others before trying to diagnose or advise. I also use my eyes and heart to listen.*
- *Right wrongs — I apologize quickly and correct errors when possible.*
- *Show loyalty — I give credit to others. I speak about and defend others as if they are present. I do not disclose confidential information.*
- *Talk straight — I communicate clearly. I clarify expectations by creating a shared vision and agreement up front. I tell the truth and have no hidden agendas. I take tough issues head-on, and I share courageously and vulnerably.*
- *Extend trust — I deliberately extend trust, and abundantly to those who have earned it.*
- *Practice accountability — I hold myself and others accountable, take responsibility to get results that matter, and keep my commitments. I do what I say I will do — it is a symbol of my honor.*

In these last three chapters, we defined exactly what I needed to do to live my three core values: *Relationships, Health, and My best self.* Every Sunday I would re-read my envisioned daily behaviors and attitudes to see if I had been true to what I said was most important to me. If I did not do what I had spelled out I would do, I tried to figure out why, learn from it, and promise myself to do better the following week. If I had failed in my actions on the same issue several weeks in a row, would I need to reassess? Was what I had proclaimed to be important to me really very important after all?

There was another benefit to spelling out my core values exactly. I could more easily evaluate my daily activities as being a high or low level of importance and place them in the correct quadrant of my time management quadrant tool. This resulted in more time for Quadrant 2 activities, which brought me a fuller and happier life.

EXERCISE

Have you already spelled out your daily behaviors to support your first and second core values? If not, be sure to do so now. In addition, write down your third core value, then spend a few minutes identifying specific daily behaviors and attitudes that will support that core value. Once again, I encourage you to take your time and think deeply. Remember, you are taking an important step to ensure your present activities move you ever-closer to your future goals, which can bring you a fuller and happier life!

CHAPTER 14

OUT OF YOUR CORE VALUES FLOW YOUR KEY ROLES

LIFE IS COMPLICATED, and one way to get a better handle on your life is to deliberately break it down into major components, as in the most important or key roles you fulfill. Your goal is to ultimately dwindle down all your different roles to the seven or so most important ones you perform. Again, it is all about narrowing your focus to your key roles.

Why clarify your key roles? Gaining clarity on your life's roles can help you focus your time and energy on activities that matter most to you. Most likely, you are familiar with the 80/20 rule: twenty percent of your activities will create eighty percent of your desired results. Gaining clarity on your key roles — and where you spend your time — will help you lose the overwhelm and live your happiest life.

As I thought about key roles, I recognized that one important role has already been assigned to each of us, and this is non-negotiable.

Before you can take care of anyone or anything else, your first priority is to nurture, grow, and renew your main asset — you! So the first key role is always *yourself*. Each of us has four distinct dimensions: our physical, mental, social, and spiritual self. Looking at this segmentation allows us to regularly evaluate if we are investing the appropriate time and energy into each of our four dimensions to stay healthy, in balance, and to further develop ourselves.

To identify my key roles, I started by reflecting on my personal and professional life and listing all the many different roles I perform. Once I completed this list, I took a fresh look at my core values — those which I had already decided are most important in my life. I took each core value one at a time and reflected on what important role (or roles) naturally flows out of that value. Then I began to group, combine, redefine, and prioritize my roles until I had seven or so of my most important roles.

For instance, in my professional life while still running my business, one of my key roles was general manager, as in leading the day-to-day operations. Another key role in my business was being president of the company, as in looking after more long-term issues. Looking at my core values, out of "relationships" I could immediately identify key roles such as husband, father, family member, and friend. Over the last thirty years, I remember key roles also included soccer coach, church council president, or Rocky Mountain Leadership College organizer. As you can see, over time certain key roles can move in and out of your life.

It is not easy to limit your important roles to only seven or so. You might have to combine or eliminate some of them. For instance, when I was working at our company, I listed the following seven roles: Me, Husband, Father, Family, General Manager, President, and

Soccer Coach. Those roles were my priorities. As you can see, I did not explicitly list, for instance, Friends as an important role on my Weekly Planner. Of course, I had friends and we did spend time together, but it was more coincidental than deliberate. During the first twenty years we lived in our small Arkansas town, we got to know a lot of people, but only if they worked at our company, were involved with our three kids' soccer teams, or attended our church.

Today, my core value of *My best self* led me to write this book and create a brand-new role as Author. Another new role out of the same core value, is as my YPO chapter's Forum Officer. In that role, I encourage and support other YPO members to create high-trust relationships through well-functioning forums.

EXERCISE

I encourage you to take time to review what you have already clarified as most important in your life: your core values. Take a fresh look at your personal and professional life and create a list of all the different roles that flow out of your core values. Then group, combine, redefine, and prioritize your roles based on core values. Narrow down your list to the seven or so that are most important, remembering your first role is always to nurture, grow, and renew yourself.

I invite you to further clarify YOUR PRESENT situation

If you have not completed the previous exercises in this book, go ahead and do them now, so you can identify and prioritize your core values. Then spell out exactly what you mean with your core values in terms of your daily behaviors and attitudes.

Now it's time to "walk the talk." At least once a week evaluate yourself on how true you were to what you said was most important to you and how well you did in each of your key roles. Adjust the following week as needed.

Be sure to use the time management quadrant tool to prioritize all your activities, since now you know your core values and what is truly important to you. You can now confidently assign a high or low level of importance and urgency to each of your activities, ultimately creating more time for your Quadrant 2 activities. Begin to feel the steady progress of living your life more intentionally!

So far, you have created more clarity on what is truly important to you, and you are actively looking for opportunities to improve your present situation. This is helpful, but the process is not complete. The next big step is to complement your work on improving your present life by creating a clear picture of your desired future, which we'll address in the next section of this book. It is time to create the same clarity for your future life as you have for your present life. In the following pages, you will learn how to draw a clear picture of your future. What are your dreams and passions for living your life to the fullest and happiest? Keep reading!

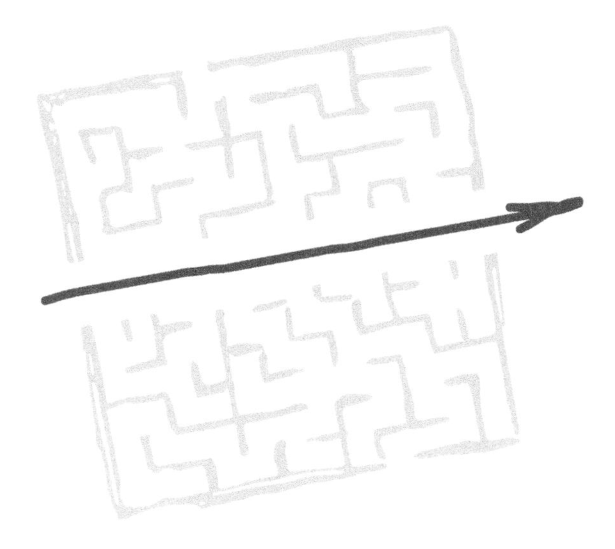

2: YOUR FUTURE

CHAPTER 15

INTRODUCTION

MAKE PROGRESS BY CLARIFYING YOUR FUTURE SITUATION

THIS BOOK IS DIVIDED into three major sections: the first segment was all about improving your *present* situation, and this second part focuses on helping you clarify your desired *future*. In the third section, I will share my *weekly process* to help you bring your present world steadily closer to your desired future. These are the major steps on the path for you to gain clarity, to live your happiest life, and for Creating Your Best You.

As you'll recall, in the first section covering your *present* situation, I shared how I learned to free up time immediately by reducing or better yet, eliminating, unimportant activities. I then shared how I created further clarity in my *present* situation by discovering and deciding what was deeply important — my values. I prioritized all these values and narrowly focused on my core values, translating each core value into specific, daily behaviors. Core values naturally defined key roles in my personal and professional life. As you completed the exercises in the first section, I hope you gained clarity on your *present* situation as well.

This second section is all about your desired *future.* I will share the process I used to discover my life's purpose and vision. As it was with my values, working on my purpose and vision was more about revealing what was already hidden inside me rather than coming up with new material.

The exercises I will share with you helped to "lift my fog." To discover my life's purpose, I looked to see where my passions, my genuine gifts (and especially those gifts amplified by my vulnerabilities), and the contributions I wanted to make all came together. Once I saw where these different elements overlapped, my life's purpose emerged. By visualizing how living both my core values and my purpose enhance each other in the future, a coherent picture emerged for my life's vision and what I could accomplish. To quote Bill Gates, "Most people overestimate what they can do in one year and underestimate what they can do in ten years."

Discovering one's purpose and vision can be daunting tasks. It makes good sense to be extra careful about who you want to become, what you want to achieve, and why you want to do that. More important than quickly climbing that ladder of success is to first make sure the ladder is leaning against the right building! We all know plenty of examples where a blind pursuit of fame, money, or power resulted in massive failures in personal and professional lives. So measure twice and cut once! I am excited to share this pathway that helped to "lift my fog." Oprah said it well with, "The biggest adventure you can take is to live the life of your dreams."

CHAPTER 16

DISCOVERING YOUR PURPOSE – YOUR PASSIONS

MY MODEL TO DISCOVER AND CLARIFY your purpose in life is to look for the one area where three things overlap: your passions, your gifts (especially those gifts amplified by your vulnerabilities), and your contributions.

Over the next chapters I will discuss in detail what is meant by passions, gifts, vulnerabilities, and contributions. I will explain the exercises for each area while sharing my own realizations as examples. At the end of the exercises for each area, I summarize my conclusions as nuggets of insight. The last step in this model is to focus on where these different insights intersect, so you can formulate a cohesive purpose statement for your life. To discover my passions, gifts, and vulnerabilities I like the exercises I learned from Jeff Manchester at Shift 180 best.

The first piece, your passions, is all about what you love to do. They energize you and make you feel alive. Personally, my passions generate a state of focus and happiness, and I feel lucky when I can act upon them. I end up forgetting all about time and naturally put more energy into my passions than is necessary. In fact, I strive to put as much heart, mind, body, and soul as possible into activities that fulfill my passions. I feel this work comes natural to me; it is as if I were meant to do this all along.

To discover my passions, I carefully pondered these questions:

1. What would you do if you had all the money and time you want? What experiences or accomplishments do you want in your lifetime?
2. If you only had six months left to live, what would you change and what would you focus on?
3. If you could solve a problem in the world or make it better, what would it be?
4. During what activities do you feel happiest, most fulfilled, and "in flow"?
5. Imagine you are 100 years old and looking back over your life. What would you have found most fulfilling?

Taking each question one at the time, I jotted down my thoughts, summarized in the following paragraphs.

1. WHAT WOULD YOU DO IF YOU HAD ALL THE MONEY AND TIME YOU WANT? WHAT EXPERIENCES OR ACCOMPLISHMENTS DO YOU WANT IN YOUR LIFETIME?

What came up for me when I was answering these questions was spending time with my children and grandkids. I want to travel with Kathy to see, enjoy, and study other parts of the world. I like learning and gaining new insights such as emotional intelligence or living intentionally. I relish helping others and "paying it forward" by sharing useful experiences. I feel I can make practical contributions by teaching others personal leadership skills that generate trust. I find satisfaction in coaching entrepreneurs, especially in the areas of finding, keeping, and developing great employees. I also feel accomplished when I am teaching kids on the soccer field, and one day I still expect to become that lean, mean golfing machine!

2. IF YOU ONLY HAD SIX MONTHS LEFT TO LIVE, WHAT WOULD YOU CHANGE AND WHAT WOULD YOU FOCUS ON?

I would spend as much time as I could with my family and friends. I would finish fine-tuning our estate planning. I would also finish and publish this book as a way to leave a legacy. For the last few years I have felt ambivalent about my Catholic religion; rather than continue to sweep this subject under the carpet, I would study and explore my own spirituality more deeply.

3. IF YOU COULD SOLVE A PROBLEM IN THE WORLD OR MAKE IT BETTER, WHAT WOULD IT BE?

I thought for years I would get involved in a noble charity and get passionately engaged. So far though, nothing has truly lit me up. In discussing this lack of a grandiose cause with Kathy, we both decided to stay open to this possibility but, for now, focus on situations where we can make a difference with individual cases.

Kathy likes to tell the starfish story. In this well-known story, a little boy and an adult are walking along the beach. Hundreds of starfishes are sweltering in the hot sun after being dumped on the shoreline by the currents and waves. The boy picks up one starfish after another and tosses them back into the ocean. After a while, the adult says, “Why are you tossing these starfish back into the ocean? You cannot possibly toss them all back or even make a meaningful difference — there are so many starfish dying on the beach.” As the little boy tossed another one back in the ocean, he said, “Well, I made a difference for that one.” So rather than waiting for something monumental to come along, we started to look around and find opportunities to help out and make small differences now.

As an example, we were able to help the former owners of our laundry, Zeke and Joan, significantly during the last years of their lives. They had no children and just a few siblings who lived far away. We regularly invited them for dinner, either at our home or at a local restaurant. After Zeke died, Joan turned inward and avoided everyone in town except us. We helped where we could and felt we did make a difference.

One day, while we were on a trip abroad, Joan had a stroke and refused medical treatment. She ended up in a local nursing home, feeling quite lonely and losing weight rapidly. Joan wanted to be near her sister, Barbara, who lived in Houston, Texas, 500 miles away. The doctor would not let her fly, and she refused to spend the money for an ambulance ride over such a distance. We asked her physical therapist to teach us how to properly lift and care for Joan, and we drove her the ten hours to Houston. Joan spent her final years feeling close and connected to Barbara. Kathy and I flew to Houston several times to visit her — always bringing a few gallons of Joan's favorite local treat, Yarnell's Homemade Vanilla Ice Cream.

Another common theme in ways I can make the world a bit better has been around helping children. When coaching kids' soccer teams, my ultimate goal was to use soccer as a way to improve their self-confidence. This inner strength could help them make smarter choices at critical moments as teenagers.

Improving teenagers' leadership skills was another way to make a difference. Kathy and I, along with our youngest daughter, Michelle, created a weeklong Rocky Mountain Leadership College for the Young Presidents Organization (YPO). In conjunction with the Outward-Bound camp in Leadville, Colorado, we developed a leadership experience for YPO kids from all over the world. The weeklong course included rappelling, white water rafting, hiking, mountain climbing, and a one-night solitary camping experience.

During breaks between the activities, I would teach "The 7 Habits of Highly Effective Teens" leadership course from Sean Covey. We never used PowerPoint presentations, had lengthy lectures, or sat in classrooms. We just spent a few minutes explaining the main principles, followed by separating the kids into small groups with instructions to come back a bit later and tell the whole group how they thought a particular theory applied to their lives.

The last big event of the week was a long hike up to a mountain summit. After dinner, all the kids received their own small tarp and were sent off to their individual camp location from 6:00 pm to 6:00 the next morning. During this solo overnight camping experience, they finished creating their personal mission statements. I wish I would have been shown and been open to absorb these seven leadership habits when I was a kid.

I like the simplicity, the immediacy, and the feeling that I am making the world a tiny bit better by creating my own starfish stories.

4. DURING WHAT ACTIVITIES DO YOU FEEL HAPPIEST, MOST FULFILLED, AND "IN FLOW"?

I loved growing and improving our small company. I was most focused on and fulfilled by enhancing our ability to attract, keep, and develop great players on our team. Naturally, this was a never-ending quest for perfection, but we saw great progress over the years by making this the core focus for our long-term success.

I felt very much "in flow" when I led our leadership team to create a clear game plan together at the end of our strategic planning process or while I taught one of our forty courses at our Searcy Laundry University. I also felt very fulfilled during my daily walks through the plant to talk to the production teammates and the delivery drivers. After talking about their families and hobbies, I would always end by asking for their thoughts on how to make our operation better or easier. My standard question was, "If you had a magic wand and you could change one thing, what would you change?" I would listen intently, make written notes, and follow up with an answer to the suggestion by the next day.

Hundreds of their suggestions were implemented over the years. Some were as simple as moving a work table a foot closer, while many other ideas were quite complex. All those changes, small and large, contributed to a well-functioning and continually improving business.

In particular, I really liked seeing and believing in the potential of one of our teammates before they did. For example, Ron was a high school graduate and was now in his late twenties. Initially, he made our logo floor mats by studying and staying focused on this new product we would provide to customers, and he had done well with that assignment and others.

As I mentioned at the beginning of this book, our company's original building structure was from the 1920s with a dozen lean-to additions. The old plant had low ceilings, wooden rafters, and a roof covered with tarpaper and asphalt shingles. Flammable fabric lint would quickly collect in those rafters, creating a real fire hazard. Once started, even a small fire would have been impossible to stop!

As we continued to grow over the years, we purchased the properties on all sides from our neighbors. We even moved our fast-growing logo mat business into a separate plant in Cabot, Arkansas, a town in the adjacent county. Eventually, we decided it was time to build a large, new, world-class plant right over the original one in Searcy. The combination of demolishing the old building, constructing a new one, and purchasing a lot of new equipment resulted in a $5 million project. Obviously, this was an extremely complicated and critical project for our small company. Kathy and I decided to put Ron in charge of this complex construction project as his sole focus. Every question, delivery, invoice, or change order went through only after Ron's approval.

As the daily laundry work necessarily continued, steel pillars for the new building would come down through the old roof and be anchored in new concrete. Slowly, we created enough support to install a new, two-story roof. All the pipes for water, steam, and air and the conduit for the electrical wiring and computer cables were suspended from the old ceiling. They needed to be carefully rehung from the new roof before we could remove the old wooden roof. It was of paramount importance to figure out the right sequence to execute the construction while keeping everyone safe and continuing to work.

Over the years I had worked hard to apply those seven habits of highly effective people from Stephen Covey to my own life, and I had indeed become more trustworthy. However, I have always had trouble with the *giving* trust part. I liked to keep close control and was always on the lookout to see how someone could abuse any of our company's systems. During the two years of the construction, Ron studied and understood every blueprint, prevented many significant problems, and allowed the rest of us to focus on our day-to-day business. I was in awe with how much better he did than I ever could have done — and seeing Ron significantly exceed his own expectations felt super gratifying to me.

Helping others achieve more of their potential makes me feel genuinely fulfilled. This construction experience also showed me how much I needed to stop trying to control everything and learn how to extend trust deliberately and abundantly to those who have earned it.

5. IMAGINE YOU ARE 100 YEARS OLD AND LOOKING BACK OVER YOUR LIFE. WHAT WOULD YOU HAVE FOUND MOST FULFILLING?

My answer: To have been a wonderful husband, father, opa, and friend. To have given it all I had to be the best I can be and to have helped others do the same. To have modeled trustworthiness, built deeply trusting relationships, and to have helped create a little of both in this world.

NOW IT WAS TIME TO BRING IT ALL TOGETHER

The next step I took was to wait a few days and answer the questions again. Where were my responses the same and where did they differ, and why? Once I was satisfied with my answers, I looked for common themes and listed all the nuggets of insight uncovered by this exercise. I clarified my passions as:

- Spending time with my family
- Helping others reach their potential
- Staying relevant by learning and constantly improving myself
- Taking care of myself physically, mentally, emotionally, and spiritually
- Developing trusting relationships
- Traveling
- Golfing

EXERCISE

To discover your passions, take time to carefully ponder the following questions:

1. What would you do if you had all the money and time you want? What experiences or accomplishments do you want in your lifetime?

___

___

___

2. If you only had six months left to live, what would you change and what would you focus on?

___

___

___

3. If you could solve a problem in the world or make it better, what would it be?

4. During what activities do you feel happiest, most fulfilled, and "in flow"?

5. Imagine you are one-hundred years old and looking back over your life. What would you have found most fulfilling?

After you have answered the questions, bring it all together — look for common themes and list all the nuggets of insight uncovered by this exercise. Make a list of your passions.

____

____

____

____

____

____

____

CHAPTER 17

DISCOVERING YOUR PURPOSE – YOUR GIFTS FROM THE "INSIDE"

IN THE PREVIOUS CHAPTER, I explained that my model to discover your purpose in life is to look for the areas where your passions, your gifts (amplified by your vulnerabilities), and your contributions all intersect and overlap. In the previous chapter, I hope you were able to identify your passions. Now let's discover your gifts!

When thinking about your gifts, look for things that you naturally excel at, do almost effortlessly, and enjoy so much you find yourself "in the zone" with time flying by. One approach, which I will show in this chapter, is to look deep within yourself for significant experiences from your past. For this exercise, I realized that I needed to listen hard to my inner voice and just start writing.

Inspiration for this process came from Steve Jobs' commencement address at Stanford University in 2005. (I encourage you to search online and read his full speech.) As he pointed out in this speech, all the twists and turns of his life were not only important but *purposeful* for his mission. He also points out that you cannot "connect the dots" at the time these events are unfolding — you can only do this with the wisdom of hindsight.

For instance, he shared his story about how he dropped out of college after just six months. However, he stayed on campus for another year and a half, only taking courses he found interesting. In a calligraphy class he learned what makes great typography great. Ten years later, when designing Apple's Macintosh computer, he knew how to design Apple's first computer with beautiful fonts.

Steve Jobs' insight was to have the courage to follow your heart, intuition, and inner voice — one way or another they already know what you truly want to become — and trust that the dots will somehow connect in your future. You cannot see this connection by looking forward, only by looking backward.

To discover my gifts, I wrote down eight significant experiences in my life, describing each one in detail and why this incident was important to me. After I wrote each story, I reflected on the skills or talents I had used during that particular event. The next step was to look for common themes among these skills and talents to recognize my true gifts. In effect, I used hindsight to "connect the dots" and get new insights on what my true gifts have been all along. Listening to my inner voice and trusting my intuition, I just started writing about these important events in my life.

I share these experiences and insights in the following paragraphs. When you reach the end of this chapter, take time to complete the exercise, so you can identify your gifts, which will help you discover your life's purpose.

"Out of your vulnerabilities will come your strengths."
— Sigmund Freud

STORY #1: STUTTERING

During my childhood and high school years, I stuttered so badly I could not finish three words in two minutes. I especially stuttered when I thought speaking well was important, for example, when I talked to people in authority, had to speak to the whole class, or was taking verbal exams.

Curiously, while I reflected on how to write down this story about stuttering as a significant experience, I noticed another, deeper set of feelings surfacing. As badly as I felt stuttering, I sometimes felt even worse *not* stuttering — when I chose to hide in the safety of staying quiet and not speaking. I felt frustrated and ashamed for being such a coward. I think even at that young age, I knew deep down each time I gave in to my anxiety by hiding, it only resulted in feeding my fear for the next time. I mostly remember a feeling of being boxed in on all sides — when I spoke and stuttered I felt shame, but when I chose *not* to speak I felt guilt.

This whole stuttering experience provided meaningful lessons for me. Stuttering and doing poorly on my verbal exams forced me to work harder for the written portions — something that was completely under my control. In effect, I found a form of inner peace in the knowledge that outworking everyone else was something totally up to me. I also learned that I needed to gather my courage, face my fears head-on, and act — or I would live with long-lasting regrets.

I saw that windows for opportunities close and, if I do not grab my chances as they arise, they might be gone forever. This realization has helped me when I faced scary, critical junctions such as whether to study abroad in the U.S. and if we should start our own company. Yes, I was definitely blessed with many wonderful opportunities, yet I also feel I grabbed these breaks quickly, wholeheartedly, and with both hands!

The specific abilities I discovered and developed from this significant life experience were my natural work ethic, persistence, courage, and urgency. My vulnerabilities around my stuttering amplified those innate talents considerably.

STORY #2: FAMILY GATHERINGS

My family was a huge part of my life when I was growing up. Virtually every Sunday after we returned from church in the morning, we would drive an hour and gather at my Opa and Oma's house — always with forty or more other family members. In addition to those weekly gatherings, there were quite a few huge family parties each year. It seemed any excuse would do to celebrate with the whole family. There were even big parties for twelve-and-a-half-year anniversaries, since that was halfway to twenty-five years!

The family always worked hard, but they made sure to carve out time for each other. Being part of this large "tribe" that often gathered together made me feel loved and secure. I learned the importance of community and prioritizing family.

STORY #3: THE SPEECH

As you may recall, I accepted the challenge as oldest grandchild to give a speech at my Opa and Oma's forty-fifth anniversary party with over 100 family members. Everyone in the audience knew me and my struggle with stuttering. My audience was almost as worried and tense as I was! I had spent several hundred hours preparing and practicing this five-minute speech, and the delivery went perfectly.

This experience was so enjoyable because, for the first time, I had faced my biggest fear head-on and had chosen *not* to play it safe. I stopped expecting the stuttering to magically go away and decided to act. With enough practice and preparation, I could create my own magic! It still makes me proud to remember that big tearful hug from Oma afterward.

My persistent work ethic and my willingness to give it all I have carried me through this experience.

STORY #4: STEPPING STONES

When I was fourteen years old, I had a good friend, Ben, who lived on the same street as I did. That summer we talked our parents into letting us go on a camping trip — just the two of us — as long as we promised to call home every night. We decided to camp on the island of Schiermonnikoog, one of half a dozen islands along the northern coast of the Netherlands.

To get to the island we had to bike to the ferry at Lauwersoog, Groningen. This was over 100 miles away, and the last ferry left at 4:00 p.m. We thought that was pretty far, but my dad said we should be able to make it with time to spare. Of course, I took that as a challenge!

So one summer morning at 5:00 we waived goodbye to our parents and took off on our bicycles for our big adventure. I remember how we had to lean forward over our bicycles' handlebars to counter the heavy weight of the saddlebags mounted over our rear wheels. The saddle bags were filled to the top and flared out as wide as they could to carry all our camping gear and luggage.

Stormy weather rolled in, and the westerly wind picked up to twenty-five to thirty miles an hour. Fortunately, the wind was at our back, and we flew along the countryside, making record time for the first sixty miles or so. When we were halfway across the Afsluitdijk, a twenty-mile-long dike along the northern part of the Netherlands, our wide saddlebags collided, sending each of us in opposite directions. Ben smashed into the railing, hitting his knee, which quickly swelled to the size of a grapefruit. He could not bike anymore, but I refused to quit and go home. We came up with a plan: I biked while Ben held his handlebars with one hand and put the other on my shoulder. This way I could pull him along while he kept his right knee still. The wind was still helping, but we were going a lot slower now.

While we struggled along, Ben suggested we change our destination to the closer island of Ameland. The ferry to Ameland left from Holwerd, in the province of Friesland, which was about twenty miles closer than Lauwersoog, which is in the province of Groningen. I was determined to stick to our original plan, probably partially motivated by my father's challenge. I promised Ben I could get us to the ferry on time. As our 4:00 p.m. deadline approached — and we could see the harbor in the distance — we got a flat tire! We quickly flipped the bike upside down, saddlebags and all, and hurriedly fixed the hole in the innertube. We ended up making the last ferry with less than five minutes to spare!

Once we ferried to the island of Schiermonnikoog, we biked the last few miles to the campground and selected our campsite as it was starting to get dark. The storm continued to worsen, and heavy rain poured down on us while we wrestled with our tiny tent in the wind. When we finally had our tent up and our luggage under cover, it was high time for our daily call home. I remember the sky turning into a strange combination of black and green colors as we biked to the one public phone on the island. Proud and tired, we gleefully told our parents that, of course, we made it safely to Schiermonnikoog.

During the night, the storm continued to strengthen, creating a rare twister, which totally destroyed the camping site in Ameland, killing three people and injuring many more. We were so glad we had stuck to our original game plan of going to the more distant island!

The next morning, we learned there was a reason the cooking equipment we had purchased was so light. The heater had one tiny flame, and it took hours just to boil a pan of water. Fortunately, our camping neighbors had watched long enough to take pity on us and let us borrow whatever we needed. During the rest of our camping stay we simplified our meals and lived on a daily regimen of grilled ham-and-cheese sandwiches. We survived our ten-day camping adventure, but Ben's knee was still swollen and painful by the tenth day. During our last call home, we asked my dad to pick us up on the mainland side of the ferry and drive us back home.

This camping trip was a significant life event, because it gave me a new level of courage and confidence. I found I could handle stepping into unknown situations — even when it felt scary at first. This camping trip turned out to be the first in a series of similar adventures, each one becoming another stepping stone to handling increasingly challenging conditions.

For instance, when I was seventeen, I spent the whole study week before the national high school final exams alone in downtown London, England, to practice speaking English to help ensure I would pass that exam. When dad dropped me off early in the morning in front of the Amsterdam Airport Schiphol, I had never flown on an airplane, been by myself abroad, or even checked myself into a hotel. This trip sounds a lot more exciting looking back than it was at the time! I often felt lonely and hesitant and had to force myself to contact strangers and speak a lot of English. The London experiment worked well, and I remember how surprised my English teacher was when I passed my final English verbal exam with flying colors the following week.

Moreover, during that week in London, I met a friendly German couple, Reinhardt and Angelika. With their help and connections, I was able to get a summer job at a pharmaceutical company in their hometown, Dusseldorf, later that year. Working by myself in Germany helped me to beef up my German language skills — essential in order to pass that class during my first year at my new college. All of these experiences strengthened my confidence, which led to embracing the opportunity to go to the U.S. when I was just twenty-one years old. I accepted an invitation to the foreign exchange study program with the University of Georgia for their MBA program. Looking back, that decision turned out to be quite the life changer!

For all these steppingstone events, the talents I used were planning and preparation. When things did not go as expected, it was my persistence and giving my absolute best that got me through. These examples show again my desire to take calculated risks and try new experiences rather than face the potential of regrets for inaction later.

STORY #5: TRUST LOST

One year while I was in high school, my ninth-grade class had gone on an end-of-year, four-day bus trip to Paris, France. The time in Paris was fun and exciting, however, this significant experience started with the bus trip back home. On this boring seven-hour road trip, I stepped out of my comfort zone and started to talk to a girl in my class, Maria. As we talked more and more, I switched seats and sat next her. During the conversation she told me she had a boyfriend who was a few years older than her. This was the first time in all the years we were in the same class that I really talked to her. We enjoyed ourselves, and after a while we started to kiss. During the long lunch break we walked hand-in-hand through the mountain park where the bus had stopped. We disappeared from sight for a while during our hike but were back before it was time to leave. Nothing else happened.

Fast-forward a couple of months to my August birthday at the end of summer break. Bart and Max, friends from school, came over to my home to celebrate my birthday. We were sitting upstairs in my bedroom, talking and drinking a few Heinekens. The topic of our class trip to Paris came up. Bart and Max were eager to know more details of what Maria and I had done while we were alone in the park. Being coy, I never *said* anything false but created the impression we had sex. They kept asking questions, and I kept giving clever answers. In a *literal* sense I did not *exactly* lie and felt that my friends' mistaken impressions were on them.

A few weeks later school started again, and Max could not wait to ask Maria about what had happened. She was surprised by the questions and, of course, denied the part about having sex. Max told the story to everyone in school, saying I was a liar. I remember asking

Bart to verify exactly what I had said. Bart told me that although he did not remember my actual words, he had the same impression as Max. Disappointed and not sure what to do, I decided not to say anything, not even to Maria, and I hoped this whole episode would quickly blow over. Well, the story did not die quickly, and school friends started avoiding me. I felt lonely and like an outsider.

A few months later on a weekend I walked into a local pub on the Zeestraat with a neighborhood friend I had not seen for a long time. As our beers were served on the horseshoe-shaped bar, I noticed Maria across the room with what appeared to be her older boyfriend. She pointed to me, and her boyfriend got visibly angry. He stomped around the bar in his heavy biking boots carrying his motorcycle helmet and a beer bottle. In my memory he was at least a head taller than me. I stayed meekly in my place at the bar, eyes down, waiting for the beer bottle to break over my head. After a moment he said, "You aren't worth it" and left. I finished my beer, said goodbye to my friend and quietly bicycled home. I felt a weird combination of relief, loneliness, shame, and stupidity.

This experience showed me how empty and superficial life is without friends. Being untrustworthy and not having the courage to own up to my mistakes created a lot of pain for myself and others. This "vulnerable experience" amplified my desire and ability to talk straight, be trustworthy, live my life with integrity, and build deeply trusting relationships.

STORY #6: TRUST SHOWN

As mentioned earlier, years ago Kathy and I were in the Netherlands to discuss financing for my still imaginary Giezeman Laundry USA. I was so eager and determined to get the financing arranged that I would have given away too much ownership of the new company. One of my uncles, Wim, insisted that everyone could only invest if they also agreed to sell their ownership stake back to us as soon as we could afford that transaction. Although Wim would be a shareholder himself, he showed more loyalty to our long-term success than to maximizing his own and the other family members' financial returns.

From this experience I began to understand how integrity and trust truly are the currencies of a leader. Uncle Wim showed me how trust is built by staying true to your values and having no hidden agendas. Looking back, I also see how much I needed good fortune and the right mentor to show up at the right time. No matter how well I prepare and study, I need to stay open to new ideas and coaches to continue to learn. Another insight from this significant life experience is that it encouraged me to look for opportunities to care for others, serving as a trusted mentor.

STORY #7: HOW TO DO TRUST

As discussed earlier, one evening I was in a bookstore at the Nashville airport while waiting for a delayed flight. This is when I discovered the book, *The 7 Habits of Highly Effective People* by Stephen Covey. After studying the book, I went to a three-day seminar and ultimately became a licensed teacher myself. I felt I had found a logical framework for how to live my personal and professional life. Most of us want high trust, and now I saw a process on how to *do* trust — how I could help create high-trust relationships and a high-trust company culture.

Certainly, my openness and eagerness to learn showed here. I love teaching and sharing my new insights. However, it is one thing to learn and something entirely different to consistently put it into practice. It was the thirty years of living and improving this new learning that made the real difference.

STORY #8: SELLING AND RETIRING

In 1997 I joined the Young Presidents Organization (YPO). Each month I met with nine other presidents of Arkansas companies for a four-hour forum meeting. The purpose of YPO forums is to meet in total confidentiality to share issues and experiences. During one meeting, I mentioned we had received two unsolicited, sizable buyout offers from large public competitors. Kathy and I had decided not to pursue the offers, since we had put our hearts and souls into our company, and we genuinely enjoyed what we were doing.

Several forum members challenged me as to why I would not even consider those offers and encouraged me to discuss the possibility of selling our company in order to further evaluate these opportunities. After sharing the facts and my emotions around this topic, other members shared similar experiences. One member was in commercial real estate. He said that when he turned down a legitimate offer on one of his properties and chose *not* to take the money offered, he in effect "bought back" this building for that price. In his view the true price of that building was now the rejected offer price rather than what he originally paid for the building. So he asked me point blank: "Jos, you said that buyout price was sizeable; would you pay that price to buy your company?" Without hesitation I answered, "No way, I would not pay one third of that price!"

Instantly, I experienced a total paradigm shift, because that one question took so many of my emotions out of the equation. If I rejected this offer, I was in effect buying my company back for this very high price by choosing *not* to take the money! Less than three months later Kathy and I had sold our company to Cintas, Inc. Of course, this was still a very challenging decision and process over an intense three-month period. Kathy and I did a lot of talking and soul searching together, and at one point we even rented a hotel room for the weekend to get away and think deeply about the offer while a house-sitter watched the kids. At the end of the weekend, we had flipchart sheets covering all the walls of the hotel room!

What would this change do to our lives — immediately and for the future? We had always told our kids, and they wholeheartedly agreed, they needed to find their own career paths outside our company. So selling our company did not breach our *family* value and would actually allow for another level of financial resources to help our family. I was also intrigued to learn more about the systems, the leadership, and the culture it takes to run a successful large public company, which aligned with my value around continuously learning and *being my best self*. This same value also meant I had to stay open to my paradigm shift.

Looking back, I know now we made the right decision, as difficult as it was at the time. Having clarity around our values helped us pick the right path during that critical fork in the road.

After the sale and payout, I chose to continue to work for Cintas at our location as the general manager. I was totally engaged and intrigued to learn how a much larger company was successfully organized. I also envisioned opportunities to help Cintas become more international by researching and potentially establishing new plants in Europe. About six months into this new job, I was feeling appreciated and receiving frequent positive feedback, but two events happened that made me change direction.

First, the fourteenth birthday of our youngest daughter, Michelle, fell on the same day in August as the corporate-wide general managers' meeting at the company headquarters in Ohio. When I worked for myself, I could set meeting dates and times around important family events. Naturally, as one of several hundred general managers my personal preferences were not really relevant. This incident snowballed into an internal debate about why I would continue to work. We had the investment returns from the sale of our company, which meant my salary was nice but not necessary. If I truly valued my family so highly and did not need the salary, why would I choose to miss out on unique family events like this birthday?

The second experience that influenced me to change my direction was a four-day YPO seminar on the Massachusetts Institute of Technology campus in the Boston area. This meeting explored the effects of major life changes. Selling our company certainly felt like a major life change, so both Kathy and I went to the seminar. Kathy had already decided to stop working at Cintas in about a year, after the computer system transition was completed. During the four-day seminar Kathy and I worked quite late each night further processing and discussing our daily exercises. We ended up focusing on why I had this need to keep working. Part of the seminar work was to slowly peel back all my protective, outside layers in order to get to my vulnerable core.

After four days of intense soul searching and challenging observations from peers, I came to a new understanding. I began to see how I believed I needed to feel and be seen as a successful executive to safeguard my ego. Without this powerful aura of prestige and importance, I might somehow return to that boxed-in, frustrated, and stuttering boy of my past.

Once I identified why I felt the need to be recognized as a successful executive, I could start to logically confront this anxiety. I was amazed at the story I was telling myself. It was so illogical, yet so powerful, because the feelings and fears were rooted in my past vulnerabilities. Almost immediately I felt my irrational fear diminishing. The following Monday when I returned to work, I turned in my six months' notice and retired from full-time work after about one year of working with Cintas.

Selling our company and retiring at age forty-six was significant, since it felt scary and unnatural, and it was exactly the opposite of how Kathy and I had planned our future. Our long-range written plan was to create a strong leadership team to run the day-to-day operations while we moved to a more strategic function, working well into our seventies. Though this was a massive change to our life plan, we chose to live true to our core values.

The ability I used through this experience was staying open to coaching and new insights. I always looked for opportunities to develop and improve. This experience further reinforced my belief in how critical it is to be clear about my values and secure enough to act on them.

THE NEXT STEP: "CONNECTING THE DOTS" TO CLARIFY MY GIFTS USING THIS "INSIDE" METHOD

Next, I looked over these stories that my inner voice picked out as being significant experiences in my life. While reviewing them, I looked for any common themes that might emerge and wrote the key insight nuggets that I discovered during this exercise. I clarified my gifts using this "inside" method as:

- Seizing opportunities to grow in order to avoid regrets later
- Being persistent, focused, disciplined, and all in
- Building trust by being trustworthy and living with integrity
- Prioritizing family relationships
- Loving to learn and becoming better tomorrow
- Living up to my fullest potential and helping others to do the same

I invite you to see what comes up for you. Write out your significant experiences. Try not to overthink it and just enjoy letting your memories and emotions flow throughout the process. After writing about your six to eight experiences, explore each one as to why it was meaningful or enjoyable to you. Find the main skills, abilities, or talents you used in each experience. Review your findings and look for themes you identified in your multiple significant experiences, just as I shared with you.

With this wisdom provided by hindsight, you can start to "connect the dots" to discover your own world-class gifts. By identifying your gifts, amplified by your vulnerabilities, you are taking the next step of the journey to clarifying your life purpose.

EXERCISE

In this step to discover your life's purpose, you will focus on clarifying your gifts (amplified by your vulnerabilities). Remember, when thinking about your gifts, look for things you naturally excel at, do almost effortlessly, and enjoy so much you find yourself "in the zone" with time flying by. Think about — and write down — about six to eight significant life experiences. As you work through this exercise, I encourage you to listen hard to your inner voice and trust your intuition. Don't overthink it — just start writing.

For each significant experience be sure to address these three points:

- A full description of one of your significant life experiences ...
- This experience was meaningful or enjoyable because ...
- The main skills, abilities, and talents you used for this experience were ...

The next step is using this "inside" method to clarify your specific skills, abilities, or talents that shine through in each significant experience. Review all your gifts and look for common themes. With the wisdom of hindsight "connect the dots" to discover and make a list of your own world-class gifts.

____

____

____

CHAPTER 18

DISCOVERING YOUR PURPOSE – YOUR GIFTS FROM THE "OUTSIDE"

IN THE LAST CHAPTER I EXPLAINED and showed with personal examples my "inside" approach to discovering my special gifts as part of my quest to clarify my purpose. In this chapter I will share a second and "outside" way I used to discover my unique talents.

I simply asked ten to twenty people who know me well for their feedback. This included family, friends, colleagues, bosses, teachers, trainers, and so forth. I wanted to get feedback from people who could see things about me that I could not see myself. We all have many blind spots and might not be aware of some of our most outstanding gifts, since they may seem so natural to us.

The "outside" process I used to get another and different look at my best gifts was straightforward. Once I selected who I was going to ask for input, I sent individual emails similar to the sample below.

SUBJECT: REQUESTING YOUR FEEDBACK

Hi ____,

I am writing to ask a favor. I am in the process of doing a deeper exploration into my personal purpose and life mission. This email is only going to a select group of people who all know me well, and I would appreciate getting your feedback.

Here's what I am looking for: In your opinion, what do you think are my top three best talents, unique abilities, or innate gifts?

Can you please spend a few minutes thinking about this and email me your top-of-mind thoughts? If possible, can you provide a brief example illustrating when I used each talent or ability? Thank you for your support!

THE NEXT STEP: "CONNECTING THE DOTS" TO CLARIFY MY GIFTS USING THIS "OUTSIDE" METHOD

Virtually everyone responded quickly and there was a large overlap with the responses from different individuals. It surprised me that most of the input I received confirmed the results I learned from my "connect the dots" exercise in the last chapter. Once I gathered all the replies, I listed all the responses, grouped similar words together, and looked for the most frequently mentioned gifts.

By far the biggest surprise was the number-one answer! Thirteen out of fourteen responses shared a gift around "genuinely caring." This was described as being thoughtful of others, having empathy, feeling understood, listening hard, coaching, and feeling connected. I never saw this particular gift in my significant event stories or the "connect the dots" exercise!

The next two gifts received the same number of votes with nine out of fourteen. One gift was "a desire to always learn and improve myself," and this was also a top gift discovered by the "inside" approach in the last chapter, which I described as "love to learn" and "becoming better tomorrow." The other gift receiving nine votes was around "being all in" with words like determination, drive, energy, and 150 percent dedication. This matches nicely with the prominent gifts identified in the last chapter around "focus, persistence, discipline, and staying all in."

Worth mentioning were two other gifts. My talent to "prioritize around a clear vision and goals" received five votes. My tendency to "stay positive and generate enthusiasm" was brought up three times. The list finished with a handful of gifts that were mentioned once such as adventurous, great at storytelling, communicates well, and being an independent thinker.

Using the "outside" method — requesting input from others — helped me to clarify my gifts as:

- Caring genuinely
- Learning and improving myself
- Being all in
- Prioritizing around a clear vision and goals
- Staying positive and generating enthusiasm

Did you notice that this list of gifts is now shorter and more to the point than the list of gifts I created using the "inside" method? Taking time to conduct both exercises can give you added clarity as you strive to discover your life's purpose.

EXERCISE

Ask ten to twenty people who know you well for feedback. This can include family, friends, colleagues, your manager, teachers, trainers, and so forth. (You can use the example email text in this chapter, customizing it to reflect your personal goals.) Using this "outside" method, you can get feedback from people who can see things about you that you cannot see yourself.

Remember, we all have blind spots, and you might not be aware of some of your most outstanding gifts, since they may seem so natural to you. Don't be shy! This is a great opportunity to get positive, objective input from others.

After receiving the feedback, take a close look at everyone's answers. Group similar responses and note the number of "votes" each type of gift has received. Now "connect the dots" to clarify your gifts using this "outside" method and write your list. There's no need to check this list against the gifts you listed using the "inside" method; you will synthesize all your responses in a subsequent chapter.

CHAPTER 19

DISCOVERING YOUR PURPOSE – YOUR CONTRIBUTIONS

AFTER IDENTIFYING your passion and gifts, discovering the contributions you want to make will give you the third and last piece of the puzzle to identify your purpose in life. Contributions are the support and assistance I can provide that are deeply fulfilling to me and truly light me up. I want to discover the contributions I can make that are valued in the world and could make a difference.

To detect my contributions, the exercise I liked best was a set of questions a friend, Dub Snider, used while studying leadership at the Stagen Leadership Academy in Dallas, Texas. Deeply reflecting upon and answering the following questions helped me to learn more about my contributions:

1. What did you dream about when you grew up?
2. What are some crucial goals you want to achieve in your lifetime, both personally and professionally?

3. What are your highest long-term achievements?
4. What impact do you want to make on the world? How can you give your gifts to the world? What are your thoughts on how you can best contribute to the world?

Sharing my answers to these four questions may offer guidance as you ponder these thought-provoking questions.

1. WHAT DID YOU DREAM ABOUT WHEN YOU GREW UP?

Early in elementary school all the kids had to write a story of what they wanted to become as an adult. All my friends wanted to become a firefighter, policeman, or professional soccer player. I wanted to become president of the United States! Being raised in a small Dutch city, I did not know anybody in the U.S. so I am not sure where that thought came from. Perhaps it was that over dinner my parents were so complimentary of the country since the Americans had just elected John F. Kennedy, a Catholic, as their new president. Of course, not being a natural-born citizen of the U.S. (and other reasons!) I could never become president of the United States. Yet fifteen years later this childhood dream helped me decide to move to the U.S.

Since I would become the fifth generation owning laundries in the Netherlands, one day starting my own laundry business seemed like the thing to do. Almost all of my dad's siblings were in that business as were his father, uncles, and cousins. Every Sunday when we visited Opa and Oma, most of the aunts and uncles were there too. It never took long before the conversation turned to the laundry business.

Furthermore, my dad frequently said I should never own a laundry, since it was too much work and risk for too little money. Dad promised to pay for any education I wanted as long as I was *not* going into the laundry business. Well, of course as a kid whatever you are *not* supposed to do becomes only more interesting! As you can imagine, another dream I had growing up was to speak without stuttering.

2. WHAT ARE SOME CRUCIAL GOALS YOU WANT TO ACHIEVE IN YOUR LIFETIME, BOTH PERSONALLY AND PROFESSIONALLY?

As a teenager, I wanted to find a way to reboot my life and live up to what I always knew I could be — self-confident, smart, and successful in business and family life. The best way I could envision achieving that was to go to America and start a new life full of opportunities with a "blank canvas." No past, no baggage, just me the way I was at that very moment.

Another crucial goal was to find the right spouse. Growing up I heard my dad frequently say, "Who you choose to marry is the only *really* important decision you make in your life. You cannot pick you parents or your kids, and you can always change careers. Nothing will have a greater impact on your happiness than picking the right spouse." Dad always ended that story with a grin on his face, saying he made *that* decision right.

Professionally I wanted one day to start my own fast-growing, profitable company that would be recognized as a world-class operation. And lastly, a lifelong goal has been to become my best self and to stay relevant by continuously learning and improving myself.

3. WHAT ARE YOUR HIGHEST LONG-TERM ACHIEVEMENTS?

To become a wonderful husband and father — and to learn to know that is enough.

4. WHAT IMPACT DO YOU WANT TO MAKE ON THE WORLD? HOW CAN YOU GIVE YOUR GIFTS TO THE WORLD? WHAT ARE YOUR THOUGHTS ON HOW YOU CAN BEST CONTRIBUTE TO THE WORLD?

I want to help build more trust in the world by modeling trustworthiness and helping to create deeply trusting relationships. Inspiring and genuinely helping family, friends, and others live their lives to the fullest and happiest would be my best contribution.

BRINGING IT ALL TOGETHER ...

After finishing this exercise around my contributions as they pertain to my purpose in life, I waited a few days and answered the questions again without reviewing my first answers. I then evaluated and explored any differences in my responses until I was satisfied with all my replies. At that point I looked for common themes and listed the important nuggets of insight uncovered by this exercise. I clarified my contributions as:

- Becoming a wonderful husband and father
- Becoming my best self by learning and practicing what I learned
- Helping to create more trust in the world, which starts by being trustworthy
- Sharing insights to genuinely help others

EXERCISE

Answer and deeply reflect on the following questions to learn more about your contributions:

- What did you dream about when you grew up?

____

____

____

- What are some crucial goals you want to achieve in your lifetime, both personally and professionally?

____

____

____

- What are your highest long-term achievements?

____

____

____

- What impact do you want to make on the world? How can you give your gifts to the world? What are your thoughts on how you can best contribute to the world?

____

____

____

Now, bring it all together by evaluating and exploring your responses. Look for common themes and nuggets of insight. Make a list of your contributions.

____

____

____

____

____

____

____

____

CHAPTER 20

SYNTHESIZING ALL THE PIECES – YOUR LIFE'S PURPOSE

TO UNCOVER YOUR LIFE'S PURPOSE, you look for areas in your life where your passions, your gifts (especially those gifts amplified by your vulnerabilities), and your contributions all come together and overlap. To synthesize your learnings first list the nuggets of insight you discovered and clarified through the exercises in the last few chapters about your passions, gifts, and contributions.

The next step is to look for common themes and similar phrases among *all three* of these different aspects of your life. Once you discover such a theme, list these expressions together and find a few key words to summarize them. Next, synthesize these few key descriptive words into a single, coherent life's purpose statement. The final act in this process is to deeply question your newly created purpose statement by asking Why three to five times. What exactly are your underlying beliefs that make this life's purpose statement so motivating and exciting to you?

As an example, I will show how I worked through this process step by step. Earlier I clarified my passions in Chapter 16 as:

- Spending time with my family
- Helping others reach their potential
- Staying relevant by learning and constantly improving myself
- Taking care of myself physically, mentally, emotionally, and spiritually
- Developing trusting relationships
- Traveling
- Golfing

My gifts and vulnerabilities discovered by using the "inside" method of "connecting the dots" with the wisdom of hindsight in Chapter 17 are:

- Seizing opportunities to grow in order to avoid regrets later
- Being persistent, focused, disciplined and all in
- Building trust by being trustworthy and living with integrity
- Prioritizing family relationships
- Loving to learn and becoming better tomorrow
- Living up to my fullest potential and helping others do the same

As discussed in Chapter 18, my gifts from the "outside" based on feedback from people who know me well were:

- Caring genuinely
- Learning and improving myself

- Being all in
- Prioritizing around a clear vision and goals
- Staying positive and generating enthusiasm

In Chapter 19, I summarized my contributions as:

- Becoming a wonderful husband and father
- Becoming my best self by learning and practicing what I learned
- Helping to create more trust in the world, which starts by being trustworthy
- Sharing insights to genuinely help others

How could I synthesize all these pieces in order to clarify my life's purpose? I first eliminated any nuggets of insight that showed up in fewer than three categories. This included golf, traveling, prioritizing around a clear vision and goals, and staying positive and generating enthusiasm. Of course, I found "prioritizing around a clear vision and goals" very important, since it is the first part of the *My best self* value. But to find my life's purpose, I focused on looking for similar phrases that showed up in all three areas (passions, gifts, and contributions) and then found a few defining words that captured the meaning of all these similar sayings:

The first group of similar phrases I found in all three areas was:

- Spending time with my family (passions)
- Prioritizing family relationships (gifts)
- Becoming a wonderful husband and father (contributions)

I captured the general meaning of these three points under the term "family relationships."

The next group of nuggets that fit well together were:

- Helping others reach their potential (passions)
- Genuine caring and helping others live up to their full potential (gifts)
- Sharing insights to genuinely help others (contributions)

I summarized the intent of these statements with the phrase "genuine caring."

There is an overabundance of words that fit well together around the third overlapping group:

- Staying relevant by learning and constantly improving myself; taking care of myself physically, mentally, emotionally, and spiritually (passions)
- Seizing opportunities to grow in order to avoid regrets later; learning and improving myself; being all in; loving to learn and becoming better tomorrow; disciplined, persistent, and focused; living up to my full potential (gifts)
- Becoming my best self by learning and practicing what I learned (contributions)

The essence of what I mean by all these statements is "continuously learning and being all in."

The last cluster of words that showed up in all three categories was:

- Developing trusting relationships (passions)
- Building trust by being trustworthy and living with integrity (gifts)
- Helping to create more trust in the world, which starts by being trustworthy (contributions)

The underlying core of these expressions is all about "helping to create more trust in my relationships and in the world."

The summary statements of the key words describing all the overlapping areas of my passions, gifts, and contributions are "family relationships," "genuine caring," "continuously learning and being all in" and "helping to create more trust in my relationships and in the world."

In setting your life's purpose, you can take a page from the business world. Create your own big, hairy audacious goal, or BHAG (pronounced bee-hag). The term was coined in the book *Built to Last* by Jim Collins and Jerry I. Porras. I encourage you to create a life's purpose statement that is easy to communicate, connects to something bigger than yourself, and excites and energizes you. As Bruce Lee said, "A goal is not always meant to be reached, it often serves simply as something to aim at." Excited and inspired, I organized my summary statements into:

MY LIFE'S PURPOSE:

Helping to build greater trust in my relationships and in the world by genuinely caring, continuously learning, and being all in.

The last step in this process of finding my life's purpose was to look back and deeply question whether all these pretty words were really true for me. Why does this purpose statement excite and inspire me so much? In particular, why did I place such a high value on trust?

I have always liked the exercise we used in our quality management work at our company where we try to get to the root of the issue by asking Why three to five times. For my first answer as to Why I want to help build trust as my life's purpose, it's because I believe trust is the "glue of the world." Our whole society, international treaties, stock markets, economies, and even money itself ultimately are all based on trust.

The next level of Why trust is so important to me brings me to my professional and personal life. In our business, I found trust to be *the* key ingredient. As an organization we focused hard on keeping our promises and to be honest and upfront with our customers. We genuinely wanted to create a high-trust relationship with every customer. Our goal was that if our customer even thought about changing suppliers, they would call us first to give us a second chance. I also clearly remember how I felt when I found myself in very low-trust environments, which I experienced during negotiations for several potential acquisitions. I felt comfortable walking away from those deals, because too much trust had evaporated.

I believe that in my business and in my family, my most important role as leader is to model, inspire, and extend trust. In my personal and professional relationships all communication and work go so much smoother, quicker, and easier once there is a high level of trust. Furthermore, I want trust in order to stay far away from those "vulnerabilities" of painful, no-trust situations caused by my actions in the past.

My last Why is about trust in myself. When I keep the promises I make to myself, I feel a deep satisfaction and inner strength. My actions become more congruent with what I say, and I gain integrity and trustworthiness. I know I cannot generate trust without being trustworthy first. I must work from my inside out. Like throwing a rock in a pond, I can produce a ripple effect by being trustworthy, thereby generating more trust and, ultimately, creating a better world.

Yes! I enthusiastically embrace, feel energized, and wholeheartedly believe that helping to create more trust is my biggest gift to share with the world.

EXERCISE

It's time for you to clarify your life's purpose by following the step-by-step process I outlined in this chapter. To summarize, you uncover your life's purpose by looking for areas where your passions, your gifts (especially those gifts amplified by your vulnerabilities), and your contributions all come together and overlap.

Start this synthesizing process by first listing your passions, gifts (and vulnerabilities), and contributions. The next step is to look for common themes among *all three* areas. Once you discover a topic found in all three areas, list these expressions together and find a few key words to summarize them. Then finish by listing all these overlapping areas by their key descriptive words and synthesize these phrases into a single, coherent life's purpose statement.

Once you have spelled out your life's purpose, question it profoundly by asking Why three to five times. What are your paradigms and beliefs that make this newly created life's purpose statement so exciting and inspiring for you? Think about this question, then write down your answers. Lifting your "fog" and seeing clearly what you want to do with your life will become a tremendous gift to yourself. You will be energized by all the good you will bring to your world. Rather than being pulled along every day in many different directions, you are proactively choosing and taking charge of your life. What can be more important? Act now!

____

____

CHAPTER 21

DISCOVERING YOUR LIFE'S VISION

CREATING YOUR VISION is all about imagining the clearest possible picture of your best future. Your vision describes what you ideally want your future to look like. Your vision conveys your dreams and aspirations in a concise way, and it energizes and inspires you to be your best self. It becomes a lighthouse for your future paths and guides your decisions and actions, providing the direction you need when other opportunities and distractions come your way.

Creating this clarity through your vision allows you to remain focused on your top priorities. Instead of getting bogged down by taking any opportunity that comes along, you naturally are more selective by having made proactive choices embedded in your vision. Ideally, you describe your vision in just one sentence. As with our work around values and purpose, less is better. Fewer topics and words create more clarity and place an increased importance on what is stated.

Another way to look at one's life vision is to view it as the answer to many deeper life questions, such as:

- What do I want to do with my life?
- What inspires me?
- Why I am here?
- What really matters to me?
- Who do I want to become?
- What would I like my eulogy to say about me? If I picture myself sitting in the back row at my funeral, what will my family, friends, and coworkers say about me? Do I like the person they are describing?
- What are the parts of my life I would like to improve?
- What is the greatest thing I could accomplish?
- In what way is the world a better place because I was here?

We need to know where we want to end up, so when we come to those critical junctures in life, we have a better chance of picking the right road.

As you can see from the deeper life questions, there is a lot of overlap between one's purpose and one's vision. After discovering our life's purpose, crystalizing our life's vision is the next logical step in the process of clarifying our desired future. To generate our life's vision, we need to take our life's purpose and integrate it with our core values. The objective is to find the sweet spot where our purpose and our values intersect with each other.

Why do we need both a life purpose and a life vision? As noble and inspiring as our purpose statement might sound, we still need a clear beacon that will help us make consistently great choices. Our purpose statement by itself could let us do meaningful and inspiring work yet lead us away from what is most important to us. For example, in my case, my purpose statement could lead me to do a lot of trust building in distant countries, spending a great deal of time building many new high-trust relationships there while ignoring my values around family.

Looking at just my purpose statement, I could "build trust in relationships and in the world" by teaching leadership classes or establishing freshwater wells in small villages in rural Africa. My purpose of "continuously learning and being all in" could lead me to overly focus on becoming a better golfer or spending half my time practicing for physical challenges like an Ironman Triathlon. By properly grounding your life's purpose into your core values, you can create that clear lighthouse, your life's vision, to help you choose the right path at critical junctures in your life.

The process of creating your life's vision is quite straightforward, and you get to build on your previous work. Review your life's purpose statement composed in the previous chapter and your core values uncovered earlier in the book. Compare both, looking for overlapping topics first. Next, work with these statements to create a succinct, one-sentence, easy-to-understand, inspiring life vision.

As a last step, you will take that one-sentence life's vision and dig deeper into who you are and what you really want to become. Finally, you will ask the Why question three to five times to validate your new-found life's vision.

Before you dive in, I will share how I worked my way through this process and then show you step-by-step how you, too, can create your life's vision.

In the previous chapters we took a systematic approach to uncover our life's purpose. When I put all the pieces together in the last chapter, my purpose became this declaration:

MY LIFE'S PURPOSE:

Helping to build greater trust in my relationships and in the world by genuinely caring, continuously learning, and being all in.

The next step is to take our work on core values and combine it with our purpose. Earlier in the book we defined what is truly important and identified the steps involved in uncovering our core values.

For this example, I will use my core values, spelled out in Chapter 9 as:

- Relationships: Highest priority on my key relationships — wife, kids, grandkids, family, and friends
- Health: to live younger, longer
- My best self: To continuously improve and to give it all I have

In looking for the areas of similarities between my purpose and core values the first obvious overlap is around relationships. In my life's purpose I talk about "Helping to build trust in my relationships by genuinely caring" and in my core values I state "Highest priority on my key relationships — wife, kids, grandkids, family, and friends." Both declarations clearly overlap significantly. In essence, my intent here is to create wonderful relationships with those closest to me.

The second apparent connection is between "continuously learning and being all in" in my purpose and my core value of "to continuously improve and to give it all I have." My intent of learning, improving, and giving it all I have is about becoming and staying relevant to those I love.

I can now combine these overlapping areas of my life's purpose and core values into:

MY LIFE'S VISION:

To be a wonderful and relevant husband, father, opa, family member, and friend.

Just as in the last chapter that focused on clarifying my life's purpose, there was one more step to take. It was to dig deeper and ask multiple times: Why? What are my underlying beliefs and views of the world that make this vision so inspirational for me? Is this what I truly strive to become or just another well intended, nicely worded statement that will disappear in a file sometime soon?

When I think about why this vision energizes and inspires me, I see the first part of my vision statement is "to be" and is obviously all about me and written in the present tense of what I want to become. I indeed believe I need to start with myself and work outward from there. Deep down, I believe I have little control over anything in this world but myself and particularly the choices I make. First, before I can become a caring, positive force rather than a liability to others, I need to take care of myself. Hence my core value "health: to live younger, longer."

I also need to develop trust in myself by keeping the promises I have made to myself. The more I trust and like myself, the more I naturally radiate caring and positivity. In my relationships with others, I deeply believe I must first be trustworthy before I can help to create that "wonderful" high-trust environment, I want to live in.

The Why around "relevant" is about my intentions of "continuously learning and being all in" in my purpose and "to continuously improve and to give it all I have" in my values and is about using my talents to the utmost. I very much want to become better tomorrow than I am today. This inner need might have started with that elementary school report card and my parents' focus on the "Diligence and Zeal" grade as discussed earlier. I also know I want to be "relevant" by sharing unique insights and wisdom when helping and caring for others.

When peeling the onion further, I recognize a somewhat immature feeling of relishing the esteem when being asked to help and mentor, especially by those I love. However, I accept that feeling and do thoroughly enjoy helping others along their path of life by sharing what I can.

Why do I talk so much about family in my vision? I believe the quality of my most important relationships is the key to generating that high-trust environment I desire. I believe no amount of fame, prestige, and wealth in my professional life could offset the pain of having failed as a husband and father. By focusing on the vision of being a loving, caring, wonderful husband and father, I need to develop certain traits, attitudes, and behaviors. Once learned, these strengths can naturally transfer to my other key roles such as grandfather (opa), family member, and friend as well as my interactions with the greater community.

After asking Why several times and reflecting deeper on my earlier stated vision, I see my vision and legacy from the inside out starting with me, extending through my family and friends and into the world.

EXERCISE

Now it is time for you to join the fun, and I invite you to review your nuggets of insight on your core values and your life's purpose. Look where these insightful statements overlap, gather the intentions behind these linked words, and compose your one-sentence, inspiring life's vision. Follow this with the soul-searching process of asking Why three to five times to validate your final life's vision to be sure it's congruent with your deeply ingrained beliefs. This is exciting work that can create much clarity in your quest to living your life to the happiest and fullest!

CHAPTER 22

CONSOLIDATE YOUR LIFE MASTERPLAN

THIS IS A TIME to consolidate all your work so far — core values, daily behaviors, your life's purpose, and your life's vision — into a single life masterplan document. This document will help you create clarity in order to live your life to the fullest and happiest. Take a moment to do this now. As an example, my life masterplan looks like this:

MY LIFE MASTERPLAN

My core values:

- Relationships: Highest priority on my key relationships — wife, kids, grandkids, family, and friends
- Health: To live younger, longer
- My best self: To continuously improve and to give it all

My daily behaviors:

- Relationships: I am present, supportive, and genuinely caring. I constantly look for new opportunities to connect and follow up accordingly.
- Health: I am intentional about everything I consume, especially alcohol. I stretch, meditate, and exercise at least five times per week. I sleep at least seven hours per night. I have a full physical exam each year. I also schedule weekly activities for my emotional, mental, and spiritual health. I am a "lean, mean golfing machine."
- My best self: I enjoy being a lifelong learner. I embrace my changing environment. I seek feedback and learn from my mistakes. Specifically I:
    - Plan weekly: I plan, execute, and evaluate against my priorities weekly. I accept and achieve results in challenging, aligned roles and dare to say a "positive no" to roles that do not resonate.
    - Demonstrate respect: I show humility. I am fair, kind, open, and civil. I modulate my intensity.

- Listen first: I genuinely understand the thoughts and feelings of others before trying to diagnose or advise. I also use my eyes and heart to listen.
- Right wrongs: I apologize quickly and correct errors when possible.
- Show loyalty: I give credit to others. I speak about and defend others as if they are present. I do not disclose confidential information.
- Talk straight: I communicate clearly. I clarify expectations by creating a shared vision and agreement up front. I tell the truth and have no hidden agendas. I take tough issues head-on, and I share courageously and vulnerably.
- Extend trust: I deliberately extend trust, and abundantly to those who have earned it.
- Practice accountability: I hold myself and others accountable, take responsibility to get results that matter, and keep my commitments. I do what I say I will do — it's a symbol of my honor.

MY LIFE'S PURPOSE

Helping to build greater trust in my relationships and in the world by genuine caring, continuously learning, and being all in.

MY LIFE'S VISION

To be a wonderful and relevant husband, father, Opa, family member, and friend.

CHAPTER 23

CREATE YOUR FIVE-YEAR, ONE-YEAR AND QUARTERLY PLANS

AFTER YOU COMBINE ALL YOUR WORK so far into a single document — your life masterplan — you are now ready for the next steps to create more clarity. Earlier on, we uncovered our core values and determined specifically what those values mean to us by defining our daily behaviors. This exercise created clarity and no "wiggle room," so we knew at the end of the week whether we lived our daily life congruent with our core values (or not). After discovering our life's purpose and life's vision in the previous chapters, we now perform a similar exercise. Do we have a planning process with clearly defined statements, so we can regularly check whether we are making progress?

There are three levels of plans to create:

1. A plan for the next five years. This plan describes what you want to accomplish toward your vision in specific statements but typically without specific deadlines. (Over time and as we enter different stages of our lives such as starting a career, becoming a parent, a grandparent, and retiring, these clearly defined statements need to be updated.)
2. An annual plan providing more specific actions and deadlines.
3. One quarterly rock: the one thing you will focus on this quarter that is both important and the most challenging to you.

These plans are all built around the 80/20 principle. We ask ourselves what are the 20 percent (or less) of our activities that make up the 80 percent (or more) of our desired outcomes? What are the critical few activities we must get right to achieve our life's purpose and our life's vision?

For the first plan, the five-year plan, start by picking a point in the future and describing the important parts of your life — your core values — and your desired outcomes by that point in time. What do you want to achieve or have happened by the end of that timeframe? You will write this longer-range plan deliberately in the present tense as if it already has happened. Thus, every time you read your plan, you are ingraining the confidence that the vision will indeed happen.

The last time I did this exercise was around my sixtieth birthday. I described my future five years out with the following list of clearly defined statements.

MY FIVE-YEAR PLAN: AGE 65

Relationships:

- Our marriage keeps getting better: trust, communication, adventure, and love.
- To stay relevant to my (grand) kids.
- Regular communications with (grand) kids as well as a week-long vacation all together every year.
- Annual weekend reunion with both sets of siblings.
- Weekly calls with mom.

Health:

- Physical: At my ideal weight, control my alcohol consumption. Strength, flexibility, and balance to golf, bike, hike, and ski.
- Mental: Stay alert. Read or listen to twenty-five books a year. Play games, especially bridge.
- Social: Maintain best friends in Arkansas with trips and golf weekends. Create new friendships in Denver through entertaining and activities.
- Spiritual: Make daily meditation and scribing a habit. Clarify my relationship with God.

My best self:

- Keep improving my emotional intelligence (foremost by staying part of my Colorado and Global couples' forums).

- Volunteer for leadership roles, or teach locally, or volunteer with the YPO organization, or …
- Keep going outside my comfort zone and facing my fears.
- Become that "lean, mean, golfing machine."

This five-year plan further illustrates what I mean specifically with both my life's vision "to be a wonderful and relevant husband, father, opa, family member, and friend" as well as my life's purpose: "I help build trust in my relationships and in the world by genuine caring, continuously learning, and being all in."

By documenting my five-year plan, I will know whether I am making progress toward my desired future or not. As you can see, less is better. I could write down more items, but these goals are the 20 percent that give me the 80 percent of my desired results. The plan is written in the present tense and has only one deadline: my sixty-fifth birthday.

The next step is to create a more specific, one-year plan. What specific actions do I want to see happening during this upcoming year? Again, what are the top 20 percent of my endeavors for the year that will give me 80 percent of my ideal outcomes? I like to use S.M.A.R.T. goals, which stands for Specific, Measurable, Achievable, Relevant, and Time-specific. I create my one-year plan each year around my birthday for the following year. I reflect back on last year's plan, highlight what I accomplished, and review items left undone. I ask myself:

- Why was that item left undone and what insights does that provide?
- Am I "walking the talk" of my life masterplan or not?
- What do I need to adjust?

As an example, my most recent one-year plan follows.

MY ANNUAL PLAN: AGE 61

Relationships:

- Our marriage keeps getting better: trust, communication, adventure, and love. At least once a week we do something special with just the two of us.
- We find opportunities to bring our family together this summer, for example, we rent a vacation house large enough for our family and the "in-law parents" too.
- I connect with my Dutch family in the Netherlands with two to three visits this year.
- I Skype with mom each Sunday morning.
- I maintain my best Arkansas friendships with two annual golf trips, shared vacations, and their visits to Denver this year.
- I create new friendships in Denver through entertaining and activities.
- We select our long-term financial planners, accountants, and lawyers and start updating our estate plan this year.

Health:

- I have achieved my weight goal of 198 pounds. I feel good about myself and have high energy.
- I am able to play and improve in activities such as golfing, biking, hiking, and skiing. I participate in at least one organized biking event, and my golf handicap is below 10.
- I am mentally alert and challenged. I read or listen to twenty-five books this year. I play games and study bridge daily.

- Meditation is a daily habit. Each day I write down at least three things I am grateful for and visualize what I can do to make my day great.
- I have a new family doctor and have had a full medical exam.

My best self:

- I keep improving my emotional intelligence by learning from my Colorado and global couples' forums and my readings.
- I volunteer for leadership roles and teach or coach for various organizations.
- I share my insights enthusiastically with my friends and invite coaching opportunities.
- I am exploring opportunities to get involved in charitable organizations or events.

As you can see, the one-year plan is congruent with the five-year plan. Some goals are identical. Yet there are more specific details and deadlines throughout the annual plan. Each week when I reread this annual plan together with my two-page life masterplan (presented in the previous chapter), I highlight any actions that are now completed and check what I can do in the coming week to make progress on the other goals. At the end of the year, I celebrate all the accomplishments and progress toward my ideal future and evaluate what happened to the items left undone.

MY ONE QUARTERLY ROCK

The third and last step in this process is about my *one* quarterly rock and daily habits. Each quarter I focus on *one* key issue I need to achieve to accomplish my annual plan, and I make this my quarterly rock. This is the *one* thing I focus on and must accomplish during the quarter. Invariably, these are Quadrant 2 activities, since they are always important to me but not urgent. One quarter I started a daily ten-minute meditation, and another quarter my rock was increasing my workout habit to at least five times every week.

I have found that many of my quarterly rocks have ultimately been based on a change in one of my habits. My daily habits have a huge impact on my effectiveness, character, and ability to progress toward the person I envision becoming. That is why we'll discuss daily habits and quarterly rocks in detail in the next chapter.

EXERCISE

Following the guidance and examples in this chapter, consolidate your work so far into your life masterplan. Create your five-year plan, then create your annual plan, and then select your *one* quarterly rock. You can start by making notes below, however, you may want to use a notebook, laptop, or tablet to flesh out your plans.

CHAPTER 24

DAILY HABITS

YOUR HABITS CONSTANTLY EXPRESS your character, often even without your awareness, and they have a huge impact on your effectiveness in becoming the person you want to be. Habits that are aligned with your life masterplan become powerful allies. It is time to see habits as a wonderful tool and start to use them to your advantage. All your work so far leading to your life's purpose, vision, and core values helps you to clarify who you want to become and why. Remember, your ultimate goal is Creating Your Best You. Start with the person you want to become and picture what good habits that person has developed — and what bad habits that person has stopped.

"Sow a thought, reap an action; sow an action, reap a habit; sow a habit, reap a character; sow a character, reap a destiny."
— Ralph Waldo Emerson

Ultimately, habits matter most because they can change your beliefs about yourself. As Johann Wolfgang von Goethe said, "What you get by achieving your goals is not as important as what you *become* by achieving your goals." By changing *what* you do, you change *who* you become. In effect, your identity will emerge out of your habits. The process of building habits is the process of becoming yourself. With each successful habit change you get certain immediate results, and it also teaches you something far more important: that you can trust yourself.

A habit is defined as a learned behavior to a specific situation that has become nearly or completely automatic. In his book, *Atomic Habits*, James Clear describes that in our daily lives we encounter a series of events starting with a "cue," resulting in a "craving," leading to our "response," which hopefully generates our "reward." Over time as we experience our cues and cravings, we try, fail, try differently, and ultimately cut out our useless movements and reinforce useful actions to get our rewards. As we learn, we form habits as simple, reliable, and automatic solutions to the problems we face regularly. Habits are behaviors repeated enough times to become automatic and are, in effect, the mental shortcuts we learn from experience, which frees up our time, energy, and brain capacity. Positive, productive habits can actually create freedom.

When you break a habit down to its main components, you can picture a habit as the intersection of knowledge, skill, and desire. Knowledge is the *what* and the *why* to do it. Skill is the *how to* do it. Desire is the *want* to do it. In order to make something a habit in our lives, we have to have all three components: knowledge, skill, and desire. Since you went through the hard work of creating your life masterplan, you already know *what* you need to do, *why* you need to do it, and that you *want* to do it. You just covered the knowledge and the desire parts of any habit. You have already done the hard part! All that is left is figuring out that last part, the skills you need to do it. Then you will have all three components to form a new, productive habit.

The good news about habits is that we have the power to change them. Since all our habits are learned behaviors, we can add good habits and stop bad ones. As author Viktor E. Frankl famously said, "Between stimulus and response there is a space. In that space is our power to choose our response. In our response lies our growth and our freedom." As humans we have self-awareness, conscience, imagination, and willpower to choose how we react to a stimulus or a "cue" or "craving." We have that unique space to push our "pause" button before we react automatically.

I have found that the long-term success of reaching many of my goals is ultimately based on a change in one of my habits. For instance, I have achieved my weight-loss goal for a quarter, but unless I change my underlying eating and drinking habits, my success is likely to be short-lived. I like this quote by author Laurie Buchanan: "Whatever you are not changing, you are choosing."

Let me share a personal example of how changing my habits worked for me early in my career. I had written in my life masterplan words similar to the ones I use now stating that I want to listen well, continuously improve, and be a lifelong learner. I remember reading in *Inc.* magazine about Caliper, an in-depth personality test for matching quality applicants to a specific job. Intrigued by this new tool, I decided to first use it on myself. After discussing my test results with the Caliper company analyst, the good news was that I did not have to fire myself as a general manager! But the bad news was that I was severely limiting my potential by being rigid and stubborn in my beliefs, thereby hurting my ability to grow.

After I swallowed my pride and did some soul searching, I began to see how, when someone had a different opinion, I did indeed immediately focus on convincing them why I was right and they were wrong. I was not trying to listen fully and stay open to other options that might offer better solutions. Often, I was just trying to power my way through the discussion, in effect, hoping to convince others and perhaps even myself. Executing inferior solutions can, over time, really impact both business and family.

One of the best ways I could think of to learn and improve (as I had stated in my life masterplan) was to start reading self-improvement and business books. But I hated reading books! Growing up I always wanted to go outside and play soccer rather than being inside reading books. In college I had to read a lot of books, which I still hated, and after graduation I was delighted not to have to read anymore. So my question was, *How do I create a new reading habit*?

I decided to "stack" this new reading habit on top of my recently developed exercise habit of working out an hour early every morning. I installed a plastic book holder on the NordicTrack ski machine and read as I worked out. It was only about twenty pages a day, since the machine would shake quite a bit. But I stuck with it, because I so clearly knew *what* I needed to do, *why* I needed to do it, and that I *wanted* to do it. All I needed was this *how* to carve out time to regularly do it. I ended up finishing a book about every two weeks and was excited each time I had a new insight that I could apply to our company or myself. Slowly, my new reading habit formed.

Of course, the more I learned, the more I realized how little I actually knew. Over time I became much more open to other ideas and became better at genuinely listening and trying to understand first before sharing an opinion. Listening better was definitely one of those few key habits that could make a major enhancement in my personal and professional life. Ever so slowly, I became more aware of my impatience, lack of empathy, and superior attitudes.

Listening well is so important and so complex. It has so many facets that it made sense for me to break "listening better" into the different, specific components and spread out mastering this new habit over time. I started by choosing as my quarterly rock to take a few minutes at least three times a day and reflect back on my most recent conversation. Did I talk too much or interrupt anyone? Just remembering to make the effort three times a day to evaluate my own listening efforts was a challenging new habit for me to form. Then the following quarter I added the step to check if I had summarized what the speaker had said to their satisfaction before replying. Making small, steady improvements on one underlying component one quarter at a time worked well.

Obviously, my listening skills are still a work in progress, but when I look back, I can truly say I have made huge leaps forward toward listening better.

When I realized I could significantly improve my listening skills, I felt I could learn almost anything once I was convinced it was important. I did have the smarts, discipline, and perseverance to acquire relevant knowledge. I just needed the time to study and then prepare and practice applying it at our company or for myself. I began to feel a sense of deep-down confidence and began to trust myself more.

CHANGING HABITS IS NOT AN EASY TASK – APPLY A SYSTEMATIC APPROACH

Realize that each time you take an action, you are, in effect, casting a vote for or against that person you want to become. Just like an election, chances are you will not get 100 percent of the votes, but you will need to get at least a solid majority of the votes to form a new, positive habit. As votes pile up you start to change the story you tell yourself. As you see the evidence you start to believe you can do it. Aristotle said, "We are what we repeatedly do. Excellence is then not an act, but a habit."

It is all about committing to tiny, sustainable, unrelenting improvements and to keep at it. Time will amplify the margin between success and failure as your behavior becomes more automatic. Recognize that good habits make time your ally, while bad habits make time your enemy.

Success here is not a finish line to cross. Success is the endless process of refinement and getting closer. Strive for progress, not perfection. Remember, taking tiny steps consistently in the same direction will create a compounding effect that results in remarkable leaps forward. James Clear in his book, *Atomic Habits*, says, "The key to changing habits is not you but your system. You do not rise to the level of your goals; you will fall to the level of your systems."

The first systemic thing about any habit you want to change is to examine the stories you tell yourself around this habit. If you can change your mental map of how you see the world, your paradigm, a major change will become much easier.

For instance, when I was considering writing this book. I told myself stories like this: "I am definitely not an author. I cannot write well enough, especially not in my second language, and I do not even like reading books! Besides, this is such a massive time commitment. And why would anyone even be interested in what I have written?

Following long discussions with Kathy and friends, I slowly began to change my stories and paradigms. I started to see writing this book as part of my purpose around building trust and my vision of genuinely helping family, friends, and others, like you, along their path. I got excited about leaving my legacy when I pictured a copy of this book in our grandkids' hands. I decided that writing this book was indeed a large, one-time investment but not trying could become a forever regret. Besides, while writing this book, I would be educating myself to another level of understanding about this exciting material.

Now with these new stories I am telling myself, this new paradigm — committing to writing three hours every workday when I am at home — became infinitely easier. By reframing my thoughts to highlight the benefits rather than the drawbacks, my new writing habit became a new, exciting, and challenging part of my life, and the habit formed almost naturally.

There are different techniques that helped me systematically create habits. One way is to pair or stack a new habit on top of an existing one as I did with reading and exercising. Another example of stacking is adding the new habit of flossing at night right after I brush my teeth. After reading *The Miracle Morning* by Hal Elrod, I started the new habits of journaling, saying my affirmation, and visualizing each day right after I finished my ten-minute daily meditation, a habit I had already established.

Another helpful technique to develop habits is to create the right environment. For example, starting a new exercise habit by getting my gym shirt, shorts, socks, and shoes out and ready for the next morning.

Or after enjoying the Searcy, Arkansas-made Yarnell's Homemade Vanilla Ice Cream way too much, I decided to create the right environment by not keeping any in our freezer anymore. I would only buy this ice cream on special occasions.

The last and arguably most important system component to establishing better habits is accountability. Establishing new habits is more about repetition than doing it for a set timeframe. You have to do the work for the habit to form. Although you might occasionally miss, make it a point to never miss twice in a row. Another way to increase accountability is to broadcast to family and friends your new habit or to have an accountability partner. You can also do something like donating to your favorite charity each time you miss.

Here's what works well for me: I increase my accountability to myself by tracking my new habit results every day. I record this on my customized Weekly Planner, keeping a running total of "votes for" and "votes against" during the quarter. I also track in a similar fashion my four most challenging "already established" habits that I started in past quarters to maintain accountability. (You will see five rectangular boxes under each day to track habits on the customized Weekly Planner, which we will describe in detail in the next section.)

Looking back at this second section of the book, you learned how to create clarity by discovering your life's purpose, life's vision, five-year and annual plans as well as your *one* quarterly rock. In this chapter, we addressed how to establish daily habits that align with your life masterplan and help you become the person you want to be.

Now that you are crystal clear about your desired future, you are ready to act deliberately. In the third and final section of this book, you will learn how to steadily pull yourself a bit closer to your desired future each week by creating and using your customized Weekly

Planner. As you can see in this step-by-step process, you are well on your way to losing the overwhelm and gaining clarity, so you can live your happiest life.

EXERCISE

I invite you to review your life masterplan and visualize that best version of yourself — the person you want to become — and decide which bad habits to stop and which good ones you need to add. Once you list all your habit opportunities, select the few key habits that, if changed, will create a major improvement toward that person you describe in your life masterplan. Next, prioritize even further and pick only *one* big habit to change, the habit you will focus on for this quarter — your quarterly rock.

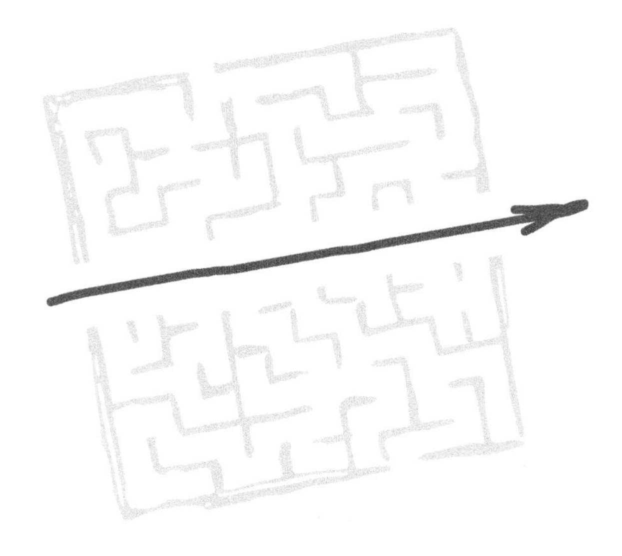

3: CONNECTING YOUR PRESENT & FUTURE

CHAPTER 25

INTRODUCTION

CONTINUE MAKING PROGRESS EVERY WEEK BY CONNECTING YOUR PRESENT TO YOUR FUTURE

IN SECTION ONE, we discussed how we could live more effectively in the present by focusing on important issues rather than urgent ones. We learned to eliminate activities in Quadrant 4 (not urgent, not important) and in Quadrant 3 (urgent, not important). Also, we recognize that we are still forced to deal with a significant number of Quadrant 1 crises (urgent, important) as they come up. However, we learned to invest time in Quadrant 2 opportunities (not urgent, important) whenever possible in order to reduce the future number of Quadrant 1 crises.

Your first Quadrant 2 activity was further clarifying what is truly important in your life. You listed what you value most and summarized this into your core values. The next step was explaining each core value in clear daily behaviors to see if you had lived your core values or not. And lastly, you defined your key roles that flow naturally out of your core values.

In Section Two, you identified your desired future by defining your life's purpose and life's vision. You found the nexus of your passions, contributions, and gifts from which your life's purpose naturally surfaced. You then combined this life purpose statement with your core values and, where they overlapped, you found your life's vision. Lastly, you created even more clarity by spelling out your desired future in detail in a five-year plan, annual plan, and your one quarterly rock. In the previous chapter, you learned how to follow up this work by creating new, productive daily habits.

Section Three is all about executing each week around your work so far and experiencing the tangible benefits from the clarity you created for yourself. In this section, you learn how to systematically integrate your PRESENT (values, daily behaviors, key roles, and Quadrant 2 activities) with your FUTURE (purpose, vision, plans, and habits) into your weekly life. Here is where you get to feel the excitement and joy of Creating Your Best You, that terrific person you always knew you could be! Even tiny steps, taken each week and in the same direction, will generate quantum leaps forward over time. Now it is time to create and use your customized Weekly Planner — an easy yet powerful tool to connect your PRESENT to your FUTURE.

CHAPTER 26

CREATING YOUR CUSTOMIZED WEEKLY PLANNER

FOR OVER THIRTY YEARS, I have continuously improved the weekly planning process I am sharing with you here. I started working with one week at a time simply because a day is too short of a period of time — all I did was reprioritize my crises! On the other hand, I found that looking at a full year, quarter, or even a month was too long of a time period; it was too far out in the future to accurately plan, adjust, and calibrate my actions while creating accountability in a way that would enable me to live the life of my dreams.

Looking at one week at a time is a perfect time period, because that is long enough to create some discretionary time slots where you can choose how to fill that time. Also, a week is short enough to easily see at a glance whether you are indeed "working your plan." A week also has a consistent rhythm, allowing you to create habits for recurring activities around certain days of the week. You can download your

Weekly Planner template with blank labels for free from our website (www.CreatingYBY.com).

Over the decades, I have found that my Creating Your Best You Weekly Planner has helped me to stay focused on my Quadrant 2 activities, my key roles, and my daily habits. This laser-focus ensures I am consistently taking small steps that, over time, result in quantum leaps toward my specific goals and, ultimately, my life's vision.

Visualize this image: You have several big rocks representing important activities (Quadrants 1 and 2). You also have a pile of pebbles representing non-important but urgent activities (Quadrant 3). Plus, you have a pile of sand representing non-important, non-urgent activities (Quadrant 4). All items need to fit in a bucket representing all your time for this week.

You can fill this bucket to the rim but not higher. If you start filling the bucket first with sand and pebbles, there is not enough space below the rim for all the big rocks. Yet if you start by putting the big rocks in the bucket first, then the pebbles can now fill in the spaces between the rocks. Lastly, you add the sand, which can now fill all the small spaces between the pebbles and rocks. Everything fits in your bucket without rising above the rim! This is essentially the process you will use with my Creating Your Best You Weekly Planner. You will start by putting in the big rocks for Quadrant 1 and Quadrant 2 activities.

First, take a moment to review the template Weekly Planner. Next, I will guide you through the process to customize your own Weekly Planner.

Creating Your Best You **WEEKLY PLANNER**

1. Me: Physical __________ 2. .... __________ 5. .... __________

Mental __________ 3. .... __________ 6. .... __________

Social __________ 4. .... __________ 7. .... __________

Spiritual __________

Sunday___	Monday___	Tuesday___	Wednesday___	Thursday___	Friday___	Saturday___

The first step to customize your Weekly Planner is to complete the top part by listing your most important personal and professional roles in your life, which you clarified in Chapter 14. In that chapter, you reviewed your personal and professional life and made a list of all your roles. As a reminder, you prioritized your roles based on what you already clarified as most important in your life: your core values. Ideally, you were able to narrow down your list to your seven (or fewer) most important roles, remembering that your first role is always to nurture, grow, and renew yourself in four aspects: physical, mental, social, and spiritual.

Showing your key roles on your Weekly Planner keeps this important information in clear view. Today, while in retirement, my seven most important roles on my customized Weekly Planner are: Me (physical, mental, social, spiritual), Parent, Spouse, Family, Friend, Author, and YPO Forum Officer.

Creating Your Best You **WEEKLY PLANNER** →

1. Me: Physical ____________
   Mental ____________
   Social ____________
   Spiritual ____________
2. Parent: ____________
3. Spouse: ____________
4. Family: ____________
5. Friend: ____________
6. Author: ____________
7. Forum: ____________

Sunday___	Monday___	Tuesday___	Wednesday___	Thursday___	Friday___	Saturday___

Now add the actual date next to each weekday for your planning week. Next, in the lines under Sunday, list up to five habits you are focusing on during this quarter. Directly under each day, you will record whether or not you successfully implemented the habit you are trying to create (or break).

Why track progress toward your daily habits? Out of your life's purpose, life's vision, five-year plan, and especially your one-year plan will come specific goals you want to achieve during this year. Some of your goals will ultimately be based on replacing some of your daily habits with better ones or even creating entirely new habits. When Kathy and I were running our company, we created a weekly key result report because "what gets measured, gets done and stays done." In a similar fashion, every morning you will reflect on yesterday's activities and record whether you successfully did the good habit you are trying to form ... or not.

Creating Your Best You **WEEKLY PLANNER**

1. Me: Physical ______ 2. Parent: ______ 5. Friend: ______
   Mental ______ 3. Spouse: ______ 6. Author: ______
   Social ______ 4. Family: ______ 7. Forum: ______
   Spiritual ______

Sunday___	Monday___	Tuesday___	Wednesday___	Thursday___	Friday___	Saturday___

Your customized Weekly Planner has space to record your performance on a handful of habits. The top line should contain the *one new* habit you decided you want to form this quarter. This might be your quarterly rock, the main thing you want to accomplish this quarter, translated into forming a new habit. The other four lines help you maintain focus on difficult habits you started in previous quarters. Follow up is key to making sure newly established habits keep on going strong.

This daily accountability of writing down your good or bad score for each habit is what makes this process work. For example, today, my one quarterly rock is around my alcohol consumption, specifically no more than two glasses of wine or beer per day. I feel drinking alcohol is the 20 percent of the input that creates 80 percent of my bad results toward my health goals, specifically my weight and sleep. I think of myself as being quite disciplined, yet I am frustrated and disappointed in myself regarding how often at the end of the day I effectively say, "screw it" and pour another glass! It is as though my "willpower battery" peters out once it gets dark outside. The next morning, when I record my result, I take a deep breath and promise myself to do better tonight. On this habit my good days still outweigh the bad ones, but just barely.

I have four other challenging habits that were my past quarterly rocks, which I record daily to help maintain them. Right now, these four habits are my daily ten-minute meditation, eating right (no junk food), exercising five days a week, and weighing myself first thing every morning (I tend not to want to weigh myself when I expect a bad result).

Creating Your Best You **WEEKLY PLANNER**

1. Me: Physical ____________
   Mental ____________
   Social ____________
   Spiritual ____________
2. Parent: ____________
3. Spouse: ____________
4. Family: ____________
5. Friend: ____________
6. Author: ____________
7. Forum: ____________

Sunday___	Monday___	Tuesday___	Wednesday___	Thursday___	Friday___	Saturday___
Alcohol						
Meditation						
Eat						
Exercise						
Weighing						

EXERCISE

It's time to create your customized Weekly Planner! Print the template Weekly Planner you downloaded from www.CreatingYBY.com. Fill in your important roles, the dates, your one quarterly rock, and any habits to follow up on. In the next chapter I will share in detail — and with personal examples — how to effectively use your one-page, customized Weekly Planner. You will learn how this simple, powerful tool helps you take small, deliberate steps toward creating the life of your dreams.

CHAPTER 27

USING YOUR CUSTOMIZED WEEKLY PLANNER

THIS IS THE CHAPTER WHERE THE RUBBER meets the road, and you learn how to "walk your talk." You will learn how to put the clarity you gained from discovering your life's purpose, life's vision, plans, values, daily behaviors, and habits steadily into practice every week. You will start to take deliberate steps toward your charted direction each week, making a real difference in your life over time. Here is where you experience the thrill of getting closer to that best version of yourself, that person you always knew you could be. Chances are you will find the peace of mind that comes from doing all you can to create the life of your dreams. Let me show you in detail how to use your customized Creating Your Best You Weekly Planner in your daily life.

First, decide on a regular day and time to work on your weekly planning process. I like Sunday mornings, but you may prefer to do it the last thing on Friday afternoons before you start your weekend or perhaps on Sunday night to plan an efficient work week. The key is to create a weekly routine that suits you best. To accommodate your preferences, I have Weekly Planner templates on our website that begin with Friday, Saturday, or Sunday.

At this regular time, I start my weekly process by rereading my two summary pages of my life masterplan (my values, daily behaviors, vision, and purpose) and my annual plan. Next, I review and evaluate my previous week using last week's Weekly Planner. I identify any listed activities I did not complete and take a moment to question why I did not finish them. If needed, I transfer any unfinished items to the following week. I also reflect on whether my behaviors last week were aligned with my declared daily behaviors that flow out of my core values. What went well? Where can I improve next week?

After rereading my annual plan and life masterplan and reflecting on last week, I am now ready to create my Weekly Plan for the upcoming week. The overall planning goal is simple: What specific steps can I schedule during this upcoming week to get me a bit closer to my life's purpose, my life's vision, my annual plan, and my one quarterly rock?

In the last chapter I shared the process to create your blank customized Weekly Planner. It's helpful to review the Weekly Planner diagram that lists my roles and habits.

Creating Your Best You **WEEKLY PLANNER** →

1. Me: Physical ________
   Mental ________
   Social ________
   Spiritual ________
2. Parent: ________
3. Spouse: ________
4. Family: ________
5. Friend: ________
6. Author: ________
7. Forum: ________

Sunday___	Monday___	Tuesday___	Wednesday___	Thursday___	Friday___	Saturday___
Alcohol						
Meditation						
Eat						
Exercise						
Weighing						

The first thing I do is take *one* role at a time and imagine how I could show up at my very best in that one role next week. What would that look like and what could I do? I then decide on *one* Quadrant 2 activity (important, not urgent) for that role. This has to be something I do not *have* to do and is not already scheduled, but something I *choose* to do. I write this *one* Quadrant 2 activity down next to that role on my Weekly Planner. Then I repeat this process for all other roles listed on my Weekly Planner.

Let me share personal examples for this particular week while I am writing this chapter. Please keep in mind I am retired now. When I was working fulltime, several roles were related to my job, and I would add one Quadrant 2 activity for each professional role.

Starting with my Me role, next to Physical I decided to choose this week's Quadrant 2 activity as doing two weightlifting sessions at the gym and three Peloton bike workouts. Next to Mental I envision reviewing sections of the *Miracle Morning* book I highlighted when I read the book earlier. Under Social I picture reaching out to our golfing friends, the Pattons, to see if they can play a round of golf with Kathy and me next Sunday and catch up over drinks afterward. For my Spiritual Quadrant 2 activity this week, I decide that I want to come up with three things I am grateful for the first thing every morning while I make a pot of coffee and look out at the snow-covered peaks of the Rocky Mountain Front Range.

My second role is Parent. The next big event as a parent coming up is a scheduled week in Hawaii with our daughter Laura, her husband, and their two young sons. For my Quadrant 2 activity this week, I plan to set aside one hour to read *Oahu Revealed* and start to outline a game plan to make this a wonderful week together.

As another example, under the role of Author I refer to my goal in my annual plan to write three hours each workday when I am at home. This upcoming week includes a holiday, so I have only four days of writing this week. Four days times three hours equals twelve hours of writing — or twenty-four half-hour *pomodoro* writing sessions. This time-management technique developed by Francesco Cirillo uses a timer to break down *pomodoros* — thirty-minute periods of highly focused work. (*Pomodoro* is Italian for tomato; he named this technique after the tomato-shaped kitchen timer he used as a university student.)

As you can see, it takes just a few minutes to list specific Quadrant 2 activities for each of your roles. Take a moment to review my Weekly Planner that lists an activity next to each role.

Creating Your Best You **WEEKLY PLANNER**

1. Me: Physical *2x Weights, 3x Peloton*
   Mental *Miracle M highlighted*
   Social *Set up golf w Pattons*
   Spiritual *Daily 3x grateful*
2. Parent: *Oahu planning*
3. Spouse: *Plan New Year's Eve dinner*
4. Family: *Mail pictures to Mom*
5. Friend: *Breakfast Bahman*
6. Author: *24 Pomodoros*
7. Forum: *First draft Transition seminar*

The next step is to open your calendar and fill in all your scheduled appointments. As you can see on the Weekly Planner, each day has its own vertical column. Your scheduled appointments will be listed directly below the habits you have listed. As an example, refer to my Weekly Planner showing my roles, Quadrant 2 activities, list of habits, and scheduled appointments.

Creating Your Best You **WEEKLY PLANNER**

1. Me: Physical *2x Weights, 3x Peloton*
   Mental *Miracle M highlighted*
   Social *Set up golf w Pattons*
   Spiritual *Daily 3x grateful*
2. Parent: *Oahu planning*
3. Spouse: *Plan New Year's Eve dinner*
4. Family: *Mail pictures to Mom*
5. Friend: *Breakfast Bahman*
6. Author: *24 Pomodoros*
7. Forum: *First draft Transition seminar*

Sunday 27	Monday 28	Tuesday 29	Wednesday 30	Thursday 31	Friday 1	Saturday 2
Alcohol						
Meditation						
Eat						
Exercise						
Weighing						
8 Weekly planner *9 Skype Mom*	*7 Meet Bob* *8 Meet Jerry* *11 Closing refinancing*	*7 Virtual exercise class Ben* *10 Zoom Tom* *3 Practice golf* *4 Golf class Tim* *6 Zoom wine tasting*	*9 Skype Mom* *10 Leave for golf + Mail pictures Mom* *11 Tee time golf with DK*	*New Years Eve* *11 Zoom Jeff on Transition seminar*	*New Years Day* *9 Skype Mom* *2 TV football Notre Dame vs Alabama*	

The following step is perhaps one of the biggest keys to long-term success. Assign the Quadrant 2 activity for each of your key roles to a *specific time slot* above the line on your Weekly Planner. This step is a critical link, since this action brings your life masterplan smack into the middle of your daily life. You identified what was most important to you in your life; now it is time to actually do it and "walk your talk"! To see an example, take a close look at my Weekly Planner showing my roles, Quadrant 2 activities, list of habits, and scheduled appointments. Notice that I have scheduled a specific time for each Quadrant 2 activity listed next to my key roles. For example, in my role as Parent, I scheduled an hour on Sunday at 1:00 p.m. to work on our Oahu trip.

Creating Your Best You **WEEKLY PLANNER**

1. Me: Physical *2x Weights, 3x Peloton*
   Mental *Miracle M highlighted*
   Social *Set up golf w Pattons*
   Spiritual *Daily 3x grateful*
2. Parent: *Oahu planning*
3. Spouse: *Plan New Year's Eve dinner*
4. Family: *Mail pictures to Mom*
5. Friend: *Breakfast Bahman*
6. Author: *24 Pomodoros*
7. Forum: *First draft Transition seminar*

Sunday 27	Monday 28	Tuesday 29	Wednesday 30	Thursday 31	Friday 1	Saturday 2
Alcohol						
Meditation						
Eat						
Exercise						
Weighing						
6 3x grateful *8 Weekly planner* *9 Skype Mom* *10 Set up golf Pattons* *10:30 Text Bahman breakfast later* *12 Peloton* *1 Ohau planning*	*6 3x grateful* *7 Meet Bob* *8 Meet Jerry* *11 Closing refinancing* *12:30 Writing 1-3 pgs* *2 Weights* *3 Writing 4-8 pgs*	*6 3x grateful* *7 Virtual exercise class Ben* *8 Plan New Year's Eve dinner* *10 Zoom Tom* *12 Writing 9-17 pgs* *3 Practice golf* *4 Golf class Tim* *6 Zoom wine tasting*	*6 3x grateful* *Print pictures Mom* *9 Skype Mom* *10 Leave for golf + Mail pictures Mom* *11 Tee time golf with DK* *3 First draft Transition seminar*	*New Years Eve* *6 3x grateful* *8:30 Breakfast Bahman* *11 Zoom Jeff on Transition seminar* *2 Peloton* *3 Writing 18-24 pgs*	*New Years Day* *6 3x grateful* *9 Skype Mom* *10 Weights* *2 TV football Notre Dame vs Alabama*	*6 3x grateful* *7 Re-read highlighted section Miracle Morning* *9 Peloton*

Now, let's discuss what goes below that horizontal line at the lower part of each daily column. This is where you place all the items you want to accomplish during the week that do not have an assigned time slot. Write the item down in the block under the day you expect to handle the issue. In addition, this space is used for anything that comes along that you want to finish this week. Here is a hint: As far as getting an item done on a particular day, I am much more flexible on items *below* the line than *above* the line. Take a moment to review my Weekly Planner with these nonscheduled items in the lower portion.

Creating Your Best You **WEEKLY PLANNER**

1. Me: Physical *2x Weights, 3x Peloton*
   Mental *Miracle M highlighted*
   Social *Set up golf w Pattons*
   Spiritual *Daily 3x grateful*
2. Parent: *Oahu planning*
3. Spouse: *Plan New Year's Eve dinner*
4. Family: *Mail pictures to Mom*
5. Friend: *Breakfast Bahman*
6. Author: *24 Pomodoros*
7. Forum: *First draft Transition seminar*

Sunday 27	Monday 28	Tuesday 29	Wednesday 30	Thursday 31	Friday 1	Saturday 2
Alcohol						
Meditation						
Eat						
Exercise						
Weighing						
6 3x grateful *8 Weekly planner* *9 Skype Mom* *10 Set up golf Pattons* *10:30 Text Bahman breakfast later* *12 Peloton* *1 Ohau planning*	*6 3x grateful* *7 Meet Bob* *8 Meet Jerry* *11 Closing refinancing* *12:30 Writing 1-3 pgs* *2 Weights* *3 Writing 4-8 pgs*	*6 3x grateful* *7 Virtual exercise class Ben* *8 Plan New Year's Eve dinner* *10 Zoom Tom* *12 Writing 9-17 pgs* *3 Practice golf* *4 Golf class Tim* *6 Zoom wine tasting*	*6 3x grateful* *Print pictures Mom* *9 Skype Mom* *10 Leave for golf + Mail pictures Mom* *11 Tee time golf with DK* *3 First draft Transition seminar*	*New Years Eve* *6 3x grateful* *8:30 Breakfast Bahman* *11 Zoom Jeff on Transition seminar* *2 Peloton* *3 Writing 18-24 pgs*	*New Years Day* *6 3x grateful* *9 Skype Mom* *10 Weights* *2 TV football Notre Dame vs Alabama*	*6 3x grateful* *7 Re-read highlighted section Miracle Morning* *9 Peloton*
Change batteries smoke alarms	*Follow up Elizabeth on estate planning. Research weight lifting coaching.*		*Check repairing ski boot.*			

The last area we need to discuss is the space right below the days of the week. Remember, in the lines under Sunday, you listed each of the habits you are working on. As you use your Weekly Planner through the course of the week, record whether you did that particular habit according to your plan ... or not. The simple act of writing down YES or NO and keeping a running score for the quarter creates a strong personal accountability, which can help you gain momentum to keep working on that habit. For example, on Monday, I have a YES for meeting my alcohol habit goal. The running score for the quarter improved to fifty-one YES votes over thirty-eight NO votes.

Creating Your Best You **WEEKLY PLANNER**

1.	Me:	Physical	*2x Weights, 3x Peloton*	2. Parent:	*Oahu planning*	5. Friend:	*Breakfast Bahman*
		Mental	*Miracle M highlighted*	3. Spouse:	*Plan New Year's Eve dinner*	6. Author:	*24 Pomodoros*
		Social	*Set up golf w Pattons*	4. Family:	*Mail pictures to Mom*	7. Forum:	*First draft Transition seminar*
		Spiritual	*Daily 3x grateful*				

Sunday *27*	Monday *28*	Tuesday *29*	Wednesday *30*	Thursday *31*	Friday *1*	Saturday *2*
Alcohol N 50/38	Y 51/38	Y 52/38	Y 53/38	Y 54/38		
Meditation Y 88/0	Y 89/0	Y 90/0	Y 91/0	Y 92/0		
Eat N 56/32	Y 57/32	Y 58/32	N 58/33	Y 59/33		
Exercise Y 75/13	Y 76/13	N 76/14	Y 77/14	Y 78/14		
Weighing Y 83/5	Y 84/5	Y 85/5	Y 86/5	Y 87/5		
6 3x grateful *8 Weekly planner* *9 Skype Mom* *10 Set up golf Pattons* *10:30 Text Bahman breakfast later* *12 Peloton* *1 Ohau planning*	*6 3x grateful* *7 Meet Bob* *8 Meet Jerry* *11 Closing refinancing* *12:30 Writing 1-3 pgs* *2 Weights* *3 Writing 4-8 pgs*	*6 3x grateful* *7 Virtual exercise class Ben* *8 Plan New Year's Eve dinner* *10 Zoom Tom* *12 Writing 9-17 pgs* *3 Practice golf* *4 Golf class Tim* *6 Zoom wine tasting*	*6 3x grateful* *Print pictures Mom* *9 Skype Mom* *10 Leave for golf + Mail pictures Mom* *11 Tee time golf with DK* *3 First draft Transition seminar*	*New Years Eve* *6 3x grateful* *8:30 Breakfast Bahman* *11 Zoom Jeff on Transition seminar* *2 Peloton* *3 Writing 18-24 pgs*	*New Years Day* *6 3x grateful* *9 Skype Mom* *10 Weights* *2 TV football Notre Dame vs Alabama*	*6 3x grateful* *7 Re-read highlighted section Miracle Morning* *9 Peloton*
Change batteries smoke alarms	*Follow up Elizabeth on estate planning. Research weight lifting coaching.*		*Check repairing ski boot.*			

ADDITIONAL INSIGHTS TO USE YOUR CUSTOMIZED WEEKLY PLANNER

Thirty years ago when I started this process, I definitely remember times when I felt quite overwhelmed. Work, kids, spouse, time for myself, extended family, coaching soccer, volunteering for church activities, and so forth — something had to give. On many Sunday mornings while planning my next week's activities, I could already see that I could not possibly do everything I envisioned — I would totally run out of time! How could I fit in all my Quadrant 2 activities next to all those already scheduled appointments?

The good news was I could see now, on Sunday morning, that I was overscheduling. Rather than waiting until I was drowning in the middle of my week, *this* became my moment to make proactive choices to spend my time wisely and determine what was truly important to me. Sometimes I would decide to cancel appointments I had previously scheduled for the week but now found just were not that important. A few times I came from the other direction and amended my Quadrant 2 activity, my important and non-urgent activity, for a particular role. Mind you, I still always kept my one activity per role, but I might choose an activity that was a bit less time consuming. What was important was to honor the fact that I was making steady progress in each of my key roles, no matter how small.

Over time, I clearly saw that once I set a specific appointment during the upcoming week for a particular Quadrant 2 activity, the probability that I would actually do it increased exponentially. Even on the rare occasions when I did not do that Quadrant 2 action item during a specified time slot, I would not cross it off on the planner and would keep seeing it on my planner during the rest of the week. Almost always, I ended up finding a new time period to get this important task done in that week.

Remember, all scheduled meetings and other events *beyond* this week are parked in my phone calendar. Only new appointments or issues for *this* week are written down immediately on this week's Weekly Planner. The key is to keep *everything* I want to get done this week in front of me. Once the issue is written down on the planner, I learned to trust I will come back to it at the right time later in the week. This process let my monkey mind calm down and fully focus on the *one* task at hand. No multitasking — I could just stay with the one, most important issue until I completed it.

In the early days of using my Weekly Planner, I remember not only running out of *time* but also simply running out of *space* on my Weekly Planner. When my single column for that day would get overcrowded, I made a mark on the planner's front page and continued my scribbled notes on the back page. On especially crazy weeks, as the back page filled up, I even stapled an extra sheet to my planner! Over time, I learned to better manage my time — and my expectations. Again, the key is to keep all that needs to be done this week together in one place and with me all the time. I must also admit that every time I finish one of my tasks, I still enjoy the simple satisfaction of crossing it off my Weekly Planner.

EXERCISE

Now that you understand how to use your customized Weekly Planner, it's time to put it to work! Follow the guidance throughout this chapter to complete your Weekly Planner and use it throughout the week. Remember, using this tool will help you systematically integrate your core values, key roles, and daily behaviors while moving closer to your life's purpose, life's vision, annual plans, and quarterly rock.

With your new-found clarity and focus on Creating Your Best You, there is one more big opportunity to explore: What new activities should you embrace, and which ones should you not even start? How can you be sure you are spending your time on activities that are truly aligned with your life's purpose and life's vision? Keep reading to learn how to use your Alignment Matrix in the next chapter.

CHAPTER 28

USING YOUR ALIGNMENT MATRIX TO SPEND YOUR TIME WISELY

NOW THAT YOU KNOW HOW TO CREATE and use your customized Weekly Planner, there is another significant tool, the Alignment Matrix, to help validate that you are spending your time wisely. This new tool is all about checking your activities to increase your effectiveness. The matrix makes sure you are doing the *right things* in the first place rather than focusing on efficiency, which is about doing *things right*. Armed with the clarity you created with your life masterplan, you can now much more accurately evaluate which activities to embrace, stop, or even better, never start.

As we discussed earlier, Jim Collins noted that, "Good is the enemy of great." It is easy to fall into the trap of doing "good" stuff that takes time away from doing your truly "great" activities — those that help you to achieve what is most important to you. When you reflect back, can you think of activities you said YES to for the wrong reasons or even without thinking it all the way through? Use your improved clarity to stay focused on your best opportunities to live your life to the fullest and happiest and say a compassionate *no* to all others.

Your time is your only non-renewable resource, and only you can choose to use it wisely (or not). Henry David Thoreau said it well with, "The true price of anything you do is the amount of time you exchange for it." When you say NO to a task or project that comes your way, you are only saying NO to one option. When you say YES, you are saying NO to every other option including Quadrant 2 tasks or projects that can move you closer toward Creating Your Best You. It is the opportunity cost of committing your time to a particular activity that generates the activity's true cost. Ultimately, each activity and your time commitment to it are based on your choices. So focus on how you are "spending your choices."

Business strategist Tony Robbins said it this way: "One reason so few of us achieve what we truly want is that we never direct our focus; we never concentrate our power. Most people dabble their way through life, never deciding to master anything in particular." Life is just too short not to pursue the best opportunities!

Use your new Alignment Matrix tool to evaluate all the new opportunities you are considering as well as your major existing activities. I first learned about this method from Jeff Manchester, an executive coach and author at Shift 180. For this process you score each activity on two scales. First, determine how high this activity rates from zero to ten on your purpose scale, your Why you would do this activity. Second, rank how high the activity aligns from zero to ten with your unique, world-class gifts, your How you would do this activity.

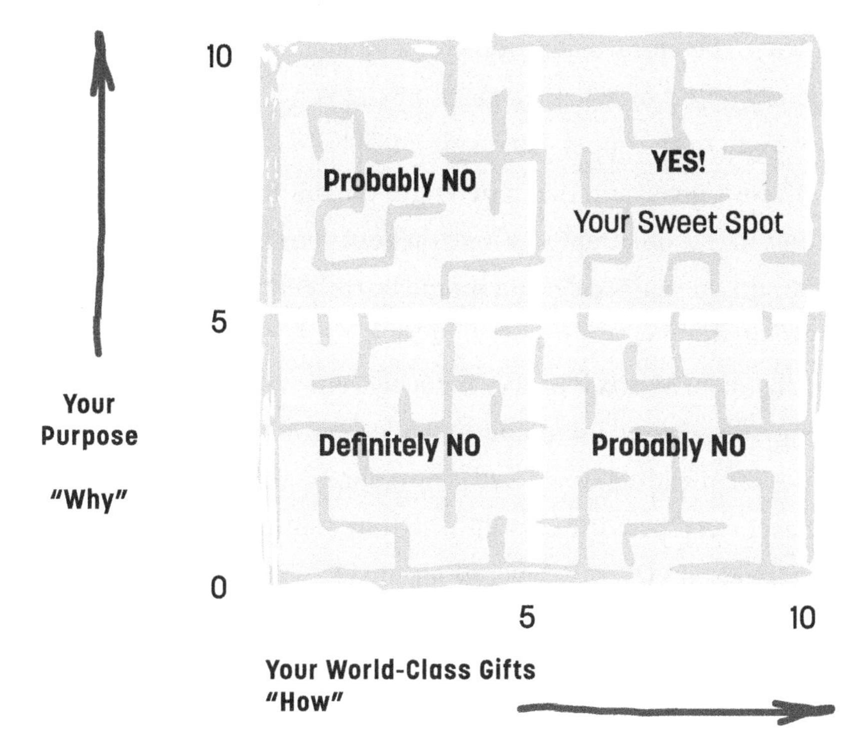

Just as we did with the time management quadrant tool, we divide the Alignment Matrix into four quadrants. Activities that rate low both on your Why and your How scales are in the lower-left quadrant. This should be a relatively simple "Definitely NO," and you should stop (or not start) these activities.

Activities that rate high on the How scale but low on the Why scale form the lower-right quadrant. We feel satisfaction when we do these activities, because we are naturally good at doing them, but these activities just do not contribute toward what we decided is important and want to create in our life.

The upper-left quadrant consists of activities that score high on the Why scale and low on the How scale. When we tackle activities in this quadrant, we end up making some progress toward our purpose and vision, but we are just not as naturally effective as others in doing these activities. Therefore, realize you probably should not do these actions. Seriously reflect on whether spending time on activities in either the lower-right or the upper-left quadrant is the best use of your time.

The last quadrant, the upper-right quadrant, is your sweet spot. Actions in this quadrant rate high on both your purpose scale as well as your unique gifts scale. You should warmly embrace your activities in this quadrant with a resounding YES! The key insight provided by the Alignment Matrix is to keep reducing your activities from the other three quadrants and increasing activities that are in your sweet spot.

Let me illustrate how I used my Alignment Matrix both to stop (or never start) activities as well as to fully commit to those that were in my sweet spot. My Why is about my purpose of building deeply trusting relationships and helping to create more trust in the world. My How comes from my unique, world-class gifts around genuine caring, continuously learning, and being all in.

With the Why on the vertical axis of the Alignment Matrix clearly defined with my purpose and vision and the How on the horizontal axis listing my gifts, I can now plot significant activities or new opportunities on this matrix.

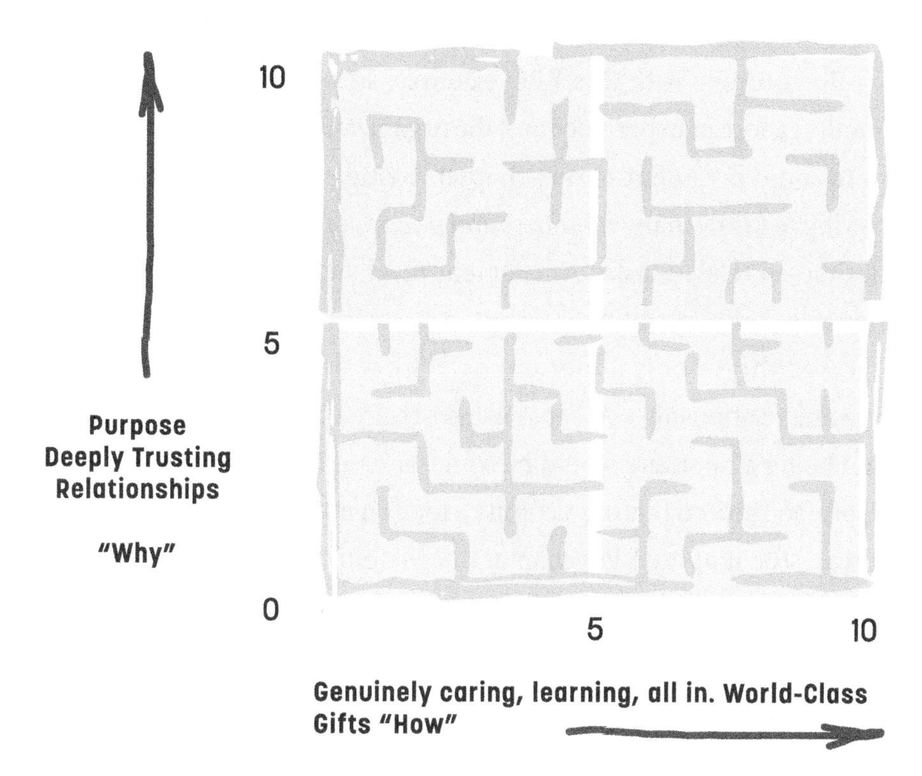

One activity is my YPO forum where eight business leaders meet for four hours every month in total confidentiality and vulnerability. The meetings are all about sharing and learning from each other's relevant experiences. As trust within the group grows, so grows the level of vulnerability when sharing business or personal issues. Over time, we are building deeply trusting relationships by adhering to specific forum procedures. On my Why scale, which is about my purpose and generating trust, this activity rates a ten. On my How scale of genuine caring, learning, and being all in, it generates a similar maximum score. This monthly event is all about caring, listening emphatically, learning, and staying totally focused. I rate this a ten on my How scale. So my monthly forum activity rates a ten/ten and is definitely in my sweet spot. You can see why there have been years when I did not miss a single meeting.

To continue with this YPO example, since I was so enthusiastic about my forum experience and the organization at large, I was asked to become president of our chapter. Being president would mean getting to know many members and potentially spending a great deal of time on related tasks. As chapter president, I would develop relationships with lots of people, but at a less intimate level. Therefore, I scored this as only a four on my Why scale with building deeply trusting relationships. As far as using my gifts around caring, learning, and being all in there would be some general learning but not much depth, so I scored this opportunity a four on my How scale. So becoming president of my YPO chapter rated a four/four on my Alignment Matrix and, therefore, it fell outside my sweet spot. So I said a caring NO to the invitation.

Notice that my Alignment Matrix provided an objective way to evaluate this opportunity. What if I had not taken time to think through the option of stepping up as chapter president? I might have felt flattered and quickly said YES. Later, when I became mired in time-consuming presidential tasks, I could have deeply regretted making the commitment.

However, becoming the YPO forum officer on that chapter's board of directors, although much less prestigious than becoming the president, rated significantly differently for me. As the forum officer my work would be around making all the forums in our chapter better, and I love helping to create that gift of participating in a well-functioning forum. Here I could potentially help others create deeply trusting relationships through training and support. I could help to create more trust. I rated this opportunity an eight on my Why scale. Since this involves genuine caring, deeper learning of the forum process, and being all in by creating seminars and innovative practices, I rated this an eight on my How scale. So being the forum officer is, for me, an eight/eight and inside my sweet spot, and I said YES to this new activity.

A few years ago, a local company asked me to join its board of directors. I felt honored, and it was a prominent job that would pay well. When I used my Alignment Matrix, I realized how unlikely it was to create deeply trusting relationships as a board member. In my past board experiences the relationships were cordial but relatively superficial. I only rated this opportunity a three on my Why scale. There would definitely be new learnings, so I rated it a seven on my How scale. With a seven/three score this board position fell outside my sweet spot, and I diplomatically declined this opportunity.

While I am not interested in jobs with boards of directors, I feel much more aligned with one-on-one coaching with the leader of a company. When coaching directly with an individual, there is a much higher potential to create a deeply trusting relationship. I rate this activity a nine on my Why scale. Coaching requires a high level of genuine caring, learning, and being all in, so I give this a high score of eight on my How scale. With a nine/eight rating, coaching business owners and top level executives falls well inside my sweet spot.

As a last example, I will share how I considered saving a lot of money by managing our family's investment accounts myself. Obviously, I genuinely care about the performance of our assets, and there is definitely a lot for me to learn. However, knowing how intense I can get with "being all in," this could quickly become a lifestyle changer. I could envision myself trying to keep up with all the relevant financial news, plus the opportunity of trying to absorb the unlimited online opinions. Once started, I would have to fully understand subjects such as options trading, derivatives, and other financial mechanisms.

I was excited about the learning opportunities in this new area, and I scored it a ten on my How scale. On the other hand, "being all in" could easily mean I would end up spending the majority of my time on this project. All this learning would happen mostly while being alone behind my computer screen. With little chance of building deeply trusting relationships, becoming my own financial manager rates a one on my Why scale. Becoming my own investor rates a ten/one on my Alignment Matrix. Therefore, this fleeting idea received a resounding NO. So I happily continue to pay the fees and evaluate our hired experts in-depth annually while staying out of this activity the rest of the year. You can see these examples illustrated on my Alignment Matrix graph.

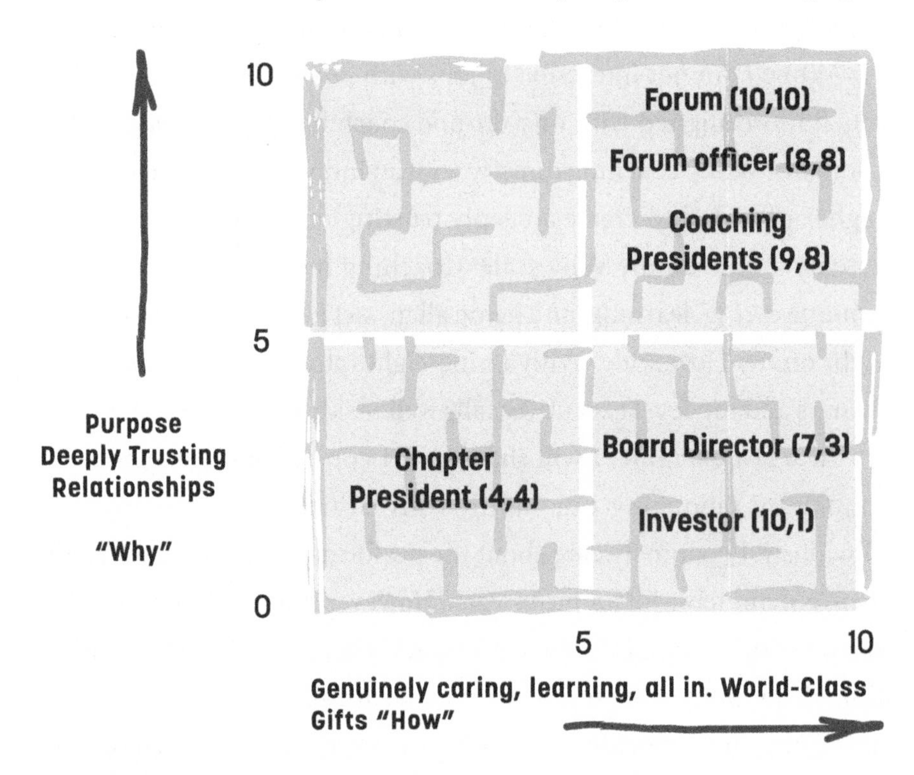

Famous management consultant and author Peter Drucker said, "Do first things first, and second things not at all." I like using the

Alignment Matrix as a tool to simplify my decisions by bringing complex issues down to what I have already decided is important to me. This simple tool shows me if I am indeed "walking my talk" and gives me peace of mind with my decisions, whether they are a YES or NO.

It is so easy to get distracted from what we ultimately want to do with our life. The Alignment Matrix — and all the other tools discussed in this book — can help you to see and stay on your path. They can help you lose the overwhelm, gain clarity, and live your life to the happiest and fullest. Think of Stephen Covey's advice, "The main thing is to keep the main thing the main thing."

EXERCISE

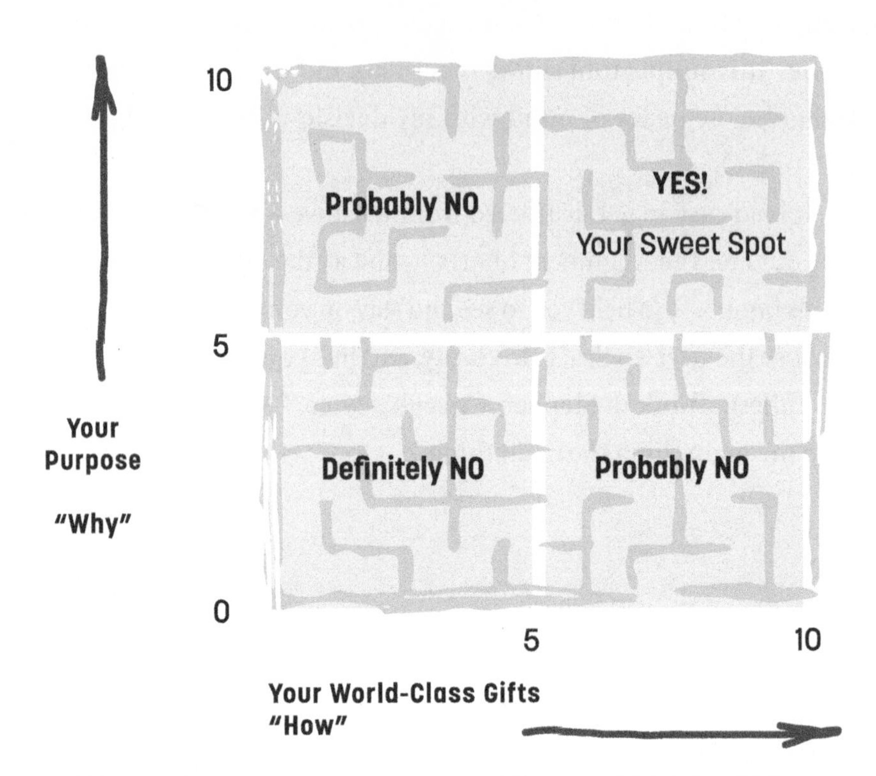

Take a minute to create your own Alignment Matrix. Write your Why on the vertical axis; this is your purpose scale — Why you would do an activity. Write your How on the horizontal axis; this indicates how well the activity aligns with your unique, world-class gifts — How you would do an activity. To start, rate your major existing activities to see where each one lands. Which activities do you want to continue? Which activities should you diplomatically stop doing, if you can? Next, practice using your Alignment Matrix for every new opportunity, task, or project that comes your way. Before you say YES to anything, always take a moment to rate it on your Alignment Matrix. Remember, this tool will help you choose how to spend your time, so you can continue to connect your PRESENT activities to your FUTURE goals.

CHAPTER 29

TIME TO START CREATING YOUR BEST YOU

CONGRATULATIONS on finishing this book! Of course, this is just the beginning and not the end. You too can lose the overwhelm and follow this step-by-step process to gain clarity and live your happiest life. Living your life in this proactive, intentional, and balanced way is so much more fulfilling than living your life day to day, feeling overwhelmed, and hoping you will somehow end up someplace good. Ultimately, the only thing you can truly control is yourself, so take charge of your life by taking the simple steps laid out in this book — and start today.

Time is the great equalizer in this world. We are all identical in that we have the same twenty-four hours each day. Time is the only resource you cannot renew, so use your time wisely. Create clarity in your life, so you can make great choices on how you spend your time. Decide what is important to you (your values), then prioritize what is of the highest importance to you (your core values). Carefully describe what each core value specifically means to you and what that looks like in your daily behaviors.

Once you clearly know what is important, use your time management quadrant tool to eliminate unimportant activities and focus on your important priorities. Then break your life up into a handful of the key roles you play and think of at least one important non-urgent Quadrant 2 goal you want to achieve this upcoming week for each role.

Following the steps in this book, you can clarify exactly how you ideally want your future to look. Like the blueprint to build a house, this mental creation precedes the physical creation. You may never reach this perfect future, but reaching for this ideal will give you a clear direction and lead you to continuously improve in important areas in the process of Creating Your Best You.

A big part of your envisioned future is clarifying your life's purpose, which you uncover at the overlap of your passions, contributions, gifts, and vulnerabilities. By combining your core values with your life's purpose, you create your life's vision. Then bring these 40,000-foot views of your desired future down to earth by creating specific, measurable, achievable, relevant, and timely (SMART) goals along timelines of five-year plans and annual plans as well as your one quarterly rock — all reinforced with your daily habit changes.

The last step is to use your customized Creating Your Best You Weekly Planner. Each week, you are step-by-step narrowing the gap between where you are now and where you want to be. Imagine the cumulative impact on your happiness when you accomplish a dozen or more well-balanced, important, nonurgent (Quadrant 2) personal and professional activities each week. Ultimately, this leads you to becoming that terrific person you have always envisioned and living your happiest life as your best you!

I invite you to start right now. Invest your time over the next few weeks to follow the exercises laid out in each step. Start to create clarity for yourself by writing your drafts, reflecting on them, and rewriting and polishing your answers as needed. The important part is to just start now.

As you spend the next weeks investing your time, consider this: What could be more important and rewarding than working on Creating Your Best You, starting to live the life of your dreams, and in the process becoming a better leader, spouse, parent, and friend? Do you remember the quote on the tomb of the eleventh-century English bishop in the beginning of this book? At his deathbed he realized, "If I had only changed myself first, then by example I might have changed my family. From their inspiration and encouragement, I would have been able to better my country, and who knows, I might have even changed the world."

EPILOGUE

Why I wrote this book

FOR FULL TRANSPARENCY, I'd like you to understand why I wanted to write this book. Once you understand where I came from, then you can understand my How and What actions as congruent with my Why. This "walking my talk" creates integrity and can lead to more trust.

As you know by now, my Why is embedded in my purpose, which is all about helping to create deeply trusting relationships and, ultimately, more trust in the world. Rather than limit myself to my family, friends, and acquaintances, by writing this book I can now potentially reach anyone, anywhere in the world. What a perfectly aligned activity with my purpose! So my main reason for sharing these insights for Creating Your Best You are to genuinely help you to live your life to the fullest and happiest. I love how my life has turned out, and I am thrilled and honored to share my story with you about how I got where I am now by using this system for over thirty years. I hope it will make a difference in your life too!

In addition to wanting to help you along your path, having to organize this material in a book format pushed me to a new level of understanding and clarity. Although I never had any dreams about writing a book, I do know myself well enough that I would have forever regretted not stepping up to the challenge to do so.

And lastly, I must admit that picturing my grandkids holding a copy of my book as part of my tangible legacy feels downright cool.

ACKNOWLEDGMENTS

I AM DEEPLY GRATEFUL for all the help and clear feedback I received from my wife of forty years, Kathy. She was always thinking along with me every step of the way in the creation of this book and cheerfully translated my written words into proper English. I also loved the input and encouragement from our son Adam and his wife, Leslie Follmer, and our daughters Laura and Michelle.

This book was kickstarted by a challenge from the affectionate Certified Forum Facilitator Jorge Cherbosque to make a presentation to our Young Presidents Organization (YPO) Global Couples Forum about why I did not want to even consider writing this book! Many thanks to the great questions and insights shared by our Global Couples Forum members: Stephen Lerer, Jane Saginaw, Dan and Margaret French, Peter and Elaine Smaller, Ralph and Trish Nagel, Diono and Mimi Nurjadin, and of course, Kathy Giezeman, which all led to a major paradigm shift on my part and to writing this book.

Along the way I received significant help and encouragement from my Evergreen Academy members Jan Burford, Rogers Yarnell, and Dub Snider. The same is true for my Rocky Mountain Gold Forum members Dave Baker, Carl Fitch, Zane Robertson, Steven Toltz, Jake Geleerd, Darius Kerman, and Mike Choutka.

As mentioned throughout this book I learned so much from many authors but especially from *The 7 Habits of Highly Effective People* by Stephen Covey, *The Speed of Trust* by Stephen M.R. Covey, and *Atomic Habits* by James Clear. I loved the exercise around values from YPO Certified Forum Facilitator Gulnar Vaswani. A special thank you goes out to personal coach and YPO Certified Forum Facilitator Jeff Manchester at Shift 180 who helped me discover several new insights and see the systemic approach embedded in this book. Thank you all.

ABOUT THE AUTHOR

JOS GIEZEMAN was born and raised in the Netherlands and received his undergraduate business degree from the Nyenrode Business University. As a part of a foreign exchange study program, he came to the United States in 1978 and received his MBA from the University of Georgia.

Upon graduation, Jos joined an industrial laundry company with plants throughout the eastern part of the United States. In 1985, Jos and his wife Kathy (who also holds an MBA) bought, with more than 98 percent debt, a small sixty-year-old industrial laundry in Searcy, Arkansas.

Over the next seventeen years, Jos and Kathy drove ever-higher levels of leadership, teamwork, and success throughout the organization. In fact, revenue grew to twelve times its 1985 level. Searcy Uniform & Mat Service was Arkansas's largest independent company of its kind and serviced more than 5,000 customers throughout the state and in the Memphis area.

Jos is a licensed facilitator of Stephen Covey leadership training. *Inc.* magazine featured a seven-page article on their Searcy company and the way Jos and Kathy incorporated Covey's leadership and time-management principles into the organization's culture.

While Covey's principles helped Jos gain clarity in business, he struggled to achieve that same level of clarity in his personal life. A health scare forced him to take stock. Jos knew he needed to find a way to clarify his personal core values, his life's purpose, and his personal vision. And he knew he needed a concrete, day-by-day method to connect his current activities to his future goals. Over the years, Jos refined these simple, step-by-step actions into a proven process, which he calls Creating Your Best You.

In 2002, Searcy Uniform & Mat Service merged with Cintas, Inc. and Jos stayed on as general manager for fifteen months before choosing to retire. Since retirement, Jos and Kathy created the Young Presidents Organization (YPO) Rocky Mountain Leadership College for kids and couples based on the Covey principles. Jos spent several years on the international Youth and Family board for YPO and has been Forum Officer in Arkansas and in Denver, Colorado, for more than fifteen years. Together, Jos and Kathy coach entrepreneurs, business leaders, and professionals in the Creating Your Best You process to guide busy, often overwhelmed, professionals to gain clarity and achieve goals in their business and personal lives.

In 2017, Jos and Kathy moved to downtown Denver. They travel extensively including to the Netherlands where Jos's family still lives. With "family" being a core value for Jos and Kathy, they make time to thoroughly enjoy their three kids and four grandchildren.

THANK YOU FOR READING MY BOOK!

Your feedback is helpful to me and to others looking for direction, so please leave a review to share your thoughts. —Jos Giezeman

Made in the USA
Coppell, TX
17 November 2021

65928159R00142